Treat Petite

42 SWEET & SAVOURY
MINIATURE BAKES

Treat Petite

Fiona Pearce

Ivy Press

First published in the UK in 2014 by

Ivy Press
210 High Street
Lewes
East Sussex BN7 2NS
United Kingdom
www.ivypress.co.uk

British Library Cataloguing-in-Publication Data
A catalogue record for this book is available
from the British Library

ISBN: 978-1-78240-098-1

This book was conceived, designed and produced by

Ivy Press
Creative Director Peter Bridgewater
Publisher Susan Kelly
Conceived by Sophie Collins
Editorial Director Tom Kitch
Art Director Wayne Blades
Design & art direction Simon Daley
Photography Sian Irvine & Clive Streeter

Printed in China

Colour origination by Ivy Press Reprographics

10 9 8 7 6 5 4 3 2 1

Distributed worldwide (except North America) by
Thames & Hudson Ltd, 181A High Holborn,
London WC1V 7QX, United Kingdom

- This book uses both metric and imperial measurements. Follow
  the same units of measurements throughout; do not mix metric
  and imperial.
- All spoon measurements are level. Teaspoons are assumed to be
  5 ml and tablespoons 15 ml.
- Unless otherwise stated, milk is assumed to be full fat, eggs are
  large and individual fruits and vegetables are medium.

Contents

There's an *Alice in Wonderland* charm about teeny chocolate éclairs, delectable miniature Victoria sponge cakes, button-like macarons... any little treats you can just pop in your mouth and finish in a bite. It's no surprise that bite-sized versions of popular bakes and desserts are the latest trend sweeping Parisian patisseries and New York bakeries. Not only are mini desserts super cute, you can enjoy them while keeping your indulgence in check!

Each chapter of this book is full of seriously adorable and delectable tiny bakes that you can easily recreate at home. Whether you fancy making lovely little sweet treats to serve at an afternoon tea party, or mouth-watering savoury morsels to impress guests at a cocktail party, there are 42 different recipes to choose from. All the recipes can be prepared without a lot of specialist equipment, and each chapter features some useful baking tips to help you achieve a professional finish. Basic recipes for the foundation of some popular bakes, such as meringue and pastry, are also included so that you can use them as a blank canvas to create your own miniature delights.

Basic Tools & Equipment

You really don't need a lot of fancy kitchen gadgets to create miniature treats, but there are a few pieces of equipment that are useful to have on hand to make baking easier and to help you achieve professional-looking results:

Pastry cutters

Small round pastry cutters (up to 5 cm/2 inches in diameter) are useful for cutting out little pieces of sponge cake, tiny biscuits and pastry rounds to make vol au vents or galettes.

Biscuit cutters

Small metal biscuit cutters in a range of shapes can be useful for cutting out treats. There are many cutter shapes available and you can easily adapt biscuit designs to make them seasonal.

Tartlet tins

Individual mini tartlet tins, 2.5 cm–5 cm (1–2 inches) in diameter, are incredibly cute and are essential for making bite-sized tartlets.

Piping bags

Disposable and reusable piping bags can be fitted with piping tubes for piping frostings, fillings and choux pastry.

Piping tubes

Piping tubes can be used to pipe meringues, fillings or frostings, or to pipe dainty choux pastry shapes. Small round or star piping tubes (no bigger than 1 cm /½ inch in diameter) are used in this book.

Squeeze bottles

These bottles are useful for making blinis or mini pancakes – they enable you to squeeze out the exact amount of liquid mixture you need. They can also be filled with thinned royal icing to flood biscuits.

Baking sheets

Lined with baking paper, baking sheets are essential for any bakes.

Mini baking tins

There are many different-shaped baking tins available and they vary in size and capacity. Mini madeleine tins and mini cupcake tins are used to create some of the recipes in this book.

Paintbrushes or mini pastry brushes

These are used for applying eggwash to pastry before baking and for dusting treats with edible lustre dust and edible gold leaf.

Non-stick rolling pin

This is an essential tool for rolling out pastry and biscuit dough.

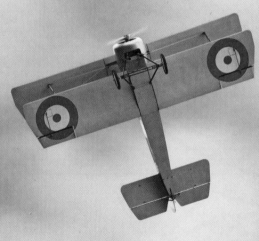

Sponges

Sponges

Sponge cakes can form a fundamental building block in your baking repertoire. If you have a regular-sized baked sponge on hand, a wide range of lovely miniature treats is only steps away.

Vanilla Sponge Cake

This recipe involves minimal preparation and produces a light, fluffy vanilla sponge.

Makes 2 x 20-cm (8-inch) round or 2 x 18-cm (7-inch) square or 2 x 30-cm x 20-cm (12-inch x 8-inch) rectangular Swiss roll tins

225 g (8 oz) butter, softened, plus extra for greasing
225 g (8 oz) caster sugar
4 large eggs
225 g (8 oz) self-raising flour
2 tsp baking powder
1 tsp vanilla extract

Preheat the oven to 180°C/350°F/Gas Mark 4. Grease the sides and base of 2 baking tins (see above) and line the bases with baking paper.

Using an electric mixer, beat all the ingredients together on a medium speed until well blended.

Spoon the mixture into the prepared tins and level out with a spatula.

Bake in the preheated oven for about 25 minutes (or about 15 minutes for Swiss roll tins), or until well risen and a skewer inserted into the centre comes out clean.

Allow the sponge cakes to cool in the tins for 5 minutes before turning them onto a wire rack to cool completely.

TIPS

Sift the flour twice to aerate it and remove any lumps. This helps create a light sponge.

Avoid taking a sneaky peek at the cake halfway through the baking time – a sudden rush of cool air entering the oven will cause the cake to sink.

ADDING FLAVOUR

You can choose from a variety of flavours to add to your Vanilla Sponge Cake mixture:
Lemon Add the finely grated zest and juice of ½ an unwaxed lemon. There is also a wide range of lemon oils that you can add instead.
Chocolate Replace 70 g (2½ oz) of the self-raising flour with sifted cocoa powder.
Coffee Add 3 tbsp cooled espresso or strongly brewed black coffee.

Vanilla Buttercream

Make your sponge cakes truly memorable with just a few swipes of your spatula. A simple buttercream recipe is all you need to start with, then add a flavouring or colouring to tailor your cakes to any occasion.

175 g (6 oz) unsalted butter, softened
350 g (12 oz) icing sugar, sifted
2 tbsp cooled boiled water
1 tsp vanilla extract

Using an electric mixer, beat all the ingredients together for at least 5 minutes until the mixture is light and fluffy. It is best to start mixing on a slow speed to prevent the icing sugar from covering the kitchen, and then gradually build up to a fast speed.

TIP

Cover the mixing bowl with a damp clean cloth while mixing the buttercream to stop the icing sugar from escaping!

Miniature Victoria Sponges

Best known in teatimes past as a 'Victoria sandwich' and first noted by the redoubtable Mrs Beeton in her *The Book of Household Management* published in 1861, this delicious sponge cake has the finest provenance and has been a favourite on tea tables all over the world ever since. Well risen, light and subtly flavoured with vanilla, these minis, like their big sister, are simply filled with whipped cream, raspberry and rosewater preserve and fresh fruit.

To make 24

1 To make the preserve, preheat the oven to 150°C/300°F/Gas Mark 2 and place a saucer in the refrigerator to chill. Place the sugar on a baking sheet lined with baking paper and put it in the oven for 10 minutes to warm.

2 In the meantime, put the raspberries in a saucepan and heat slowly, then bring them to the boil for 5 minutes. Remove the pan from the heat and then add the warmed sugar and rosewater. Stir the mixture over a low heat until the sugar has dissolved. Bring the mixture back to the boil and allow it to boil for about 10 minutes until setting point is reached. You can test that you have reached this point by spooning a little of the preserve onto the chilled saucer, allowing it to cool for a few minutes and then pushing your finger into it – if it wrinkles, it is ready; if not, return the pan to the heat and cook for a minute or two more and test again.

3 When the preserve has reached setting point, carefully ladle it into sterilized screw-top jars and twist the lids on while the jam is still hot. The preserve will thicken up as it cools and the seals on the jars should dip. If a jar doesn't seal, store it in the refrigerator and use the preserve within a couple of weeks. Sealed jars can be kept in the cupboard for months, although after 6 months the flavour will begin to deteriorate.

4 To make the filling, whip the cream with the sugar and vanilla extract in a bowl until it holds its shape.

5 To assemble the sponge cakes, use a 4–5-cm/1½–2-inch round cutter to cut out 48 rounds of sponge. Spread a thin layer of preserve on half the quantity of rounds, then spoon a little of the whipped cream on top. Scatter the chopped raspberries on top of the cream and then place another sponge round on top. Lightly dust the tops of the cakes with icing sugar before serving.

2 Vanilla Sponge Cakes, each baked in a 30-cm x 20-cm (12-inch x 8-inch) Swiss roll tin (*see page 13*)

RASPBERRY & ROSEWATER PRESERVE

600 g (1 lb 5 oz) granulated sugar

500 g (1 lb 2 oz) fresh raspberries, rinsed and drained

2 tsp rosewater

FILLING

300 ml (10 fl oz) double cream

1 tbsp icing sugar, plus extra for dusting

½ tsp vanilla extract

100 g (3½ oz) fresh raspberries, chopped into quarters

ACTUAL SIZE

Fondant Cakes

Coated with fondant icing in pink and lavender, and finished with minute chocolate motifs, only the finest bone-china tea service will match the delicacy of these delightful sponge cakes. And they taste as good as they look.

To make 64

20-cm (8-inch) square Vanilla
Sponge Cake (*see page 13*)

1 quantity of Vanilla
Buttercream (*see page 13*)

4 tbsp apricot jam, warmed

300 g (10½ oz) marzipan

100 g (3½ oz) dark chocolate,
melted, to decorate (optional)

FONDANT ICING

225 g (8 oz) fondant
icing sugar, sifted

2–3 tbsp water

1 tsp vanilla extract
(or other flavouring if desired)

pink and baby blue
food colouring

ACTUAL SIZE

1 Slice the sponge in half horizontally. Wrap and freeze one half (or use it if you would like to make a double quantity of the cakes). Carefully slice the remaining cake in half horizontally again to create 2 layers of cake, each about 1 cm (½ inch) thick. Spread a thin layer of the buttercream over the bottom sponge layer using a palette knife. Place the other half of the sponge on top of the buttercream. Brush the top and sides of the sponge cake with the warmed jam using a pastry brush.

2 Using a non-stick rolling pin, roll out the marzipan into a square about 3 mm (⅛ inch) thick, then place it on top of the cake and gently press it down with the palm of your hand or a cake smoother to ensure that it is stuck firmly to the cake. Use a knife to trim the marzipan so that it doesn't hang over the edge of the cake. Score 2.5-cm (1-inch) squares into the marzipan topping with a sharp knife. Place the sponge in the refrigerator for at least an hour, until firm.

3 While the cake is firming, make the fondant icing by mixing the sugar, water, vanilla extract and 1 drop of pink food colouring together in a bowl with a spoon until smooth.

4 Remove the sponge from the refrigerator and cut it into 2.5-cm (1-inch) squares, using the scored lines as a guide. Sit each sponge square in turn on a fork held over the bowl of icing, then use a spoon to pour the warm icing over the square, allowing any excess icing to drip back into the bowl. If desired, cover half the quantity of squares with pink icing, then mix some baby blue food colouring into the pink icing to tint it to a lavender colour and cover the remaining squares with the lavender icing. Place the squares on a wire rack to dry before putting them into petit four/mini paper cake cases. Store the cakes in an airtight container for up to 3 days.

EXTRA If desired, make small chocolate motifs by pouring melted dark chocolate into a silicone mould and allowing it to set. Flex the mould to remove the chocolate motifs and then place one on top of each cake before the icing has set.

Earl Grey Madeleines with Honey-orange Glaze

You can bake these classics in any miniature tins, but to get the distinctive fluted shape, find a mini madeleine tin online or in your local cook shop. Bite through the crisp honey glaze into the light tea-flavoured sponge and you'll find yourself transported, with Proustian accuracy, straight to a French pavement café…

To make 48

1 Grind the tea leaves into a fine powder using a mortar and pestle, then rub the sugar into the ground tea leaves with your fingertips.

2 Using an electric mixer, beat the eggs and tea-flavoured sugar together until the mixture is creamy and has doubled in size. Slowly fold in the flour, baking powder and salt until well combined. Add the vanilla extract and then gently stir in the melted butter. Cover the mixture with clingfilm and chill in the refrigerator for at least 2 hours. This allows the gluten to relax, giving the madeleines a light texture when they are baked.

3 Preheat the oven to 180°C/350°F/Gas Mark 4. Brush a mini madeleine baking tin with melted butter.

4 Spoon approximately 1 teaspoonful of the cake mixture into each hole of the baking tin to fill them two-thirds full. (Keep any remaining cake mixture refrigerated until ready to bake.) Chill the filled baking tin in the refrigerator for 10 minutes before baking in the preheated oven for 4 minutes, or until the madeleines have risen and begun to shrink away from the edges of the tin. (Keep any remaining cake mixture refrigerated until ready to bake.) Turn the madeleines onto a wire rack to cool completely.

5 To make the glaze, mix the sugar, honey and orange juice together in a bowl with a spoon. Sprinkle in the orange zest and stir until combined. Once all the cakes have cooled, gently dip into the glaze, sprinkle with more orange zest and lay them on baking paper to dry before serving.

3 tbsp loose Earl Grey tea

90 g (3¼ oz) caster sugar

2 large eggs

100 g (3½ oz) plain flour

½ tsp baking powder

pinch of salt

1 tsp vanilla extract

75 g (2¾ oz) unsalted butter, melted and cooled, plus extra for greasing

HONEY-ORANGE GLAZE

60 g (2¼ oz) icing sugar, sifted

1 tsp honey

2 tbsp fresh orange juice

1 tsp finely grated unwaxed orange zest, plus extra for sprinkling

ACTUAL SIZE

Chocolate Celebration Cakes

Light but rich, génoise sponge is a good choice for a layer cake. These featherlight miniatures are cut from a thin sheet of cake, then layered and topped with a strawberry buttercream, piped with a star piping tube to give an elegant swirled finish. Sugar roses add a suitably genteel finishing touch.

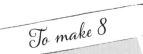

To make 8

50 g (1¾ oz) plain flour

35 g (1¼ oz) cocoa powder

4 large eggs

100 g (3½ oz) caster sugar

50 g (1¾ oz) butter, melted and hot, plus extra for greasing

sugar flowers or sprinkles, to decorate

STRAWBERRY BUTTERCREAM

2 tbsp strawberry preserve (preferably home-made but shop-bought is fine)

1 quantity of Vanilla Buttercream (*see page 13*)

pink food colouring (optional)

ACTUAL SIZE

1 To make the strawberry buttercream, stir the preserve through the buttercream until it is well incorporated. If desired, stir in a drop of pink food colouring to make the buttercream a brighter pink colour. Spoon it into a piping bag fitted with a small star piping tube and set aside.

2 To make the chocolate génoise sponge, preheat the oven to 160°C/325°F/Gas Mark 3. Grease a 20-cm (8-inch) square baking tin and line the base with baking paper. Sift the flour and cocoa powder together 3 times and set aside. Place the eggs in a large heatproof bowl and whisk in the sugar until combined. Set the bowl over a small saucepan of simmering water on a medium-low heat and whisk the mixture constantly until it is warm and foamy.

3 Remove the bowl from the pan and then whisk it with a hand-held electric mixer on high speed until the bubbles start to disappear and the mixture triples in volume. Reduce the mixing speed and whisk for a further minute. This will help to stabilize the air bubbles in the cake mixture.

4 Sift half the flour mixture into the bowl and gently fold it in until it is almost fully combined. Sift in the remaining flour mixture and fold in until it is well combined, but be careful not to over-mix.

5 Add one-third of the cake mixture to the hot melted butter in a separate bowl. Use a small spatula to fold the butter thoroughly into the cake mixture. Pour this back into the bulk of the cake mixture and fold in gently. Spoon the cake mixture into the prepared baking tin. Tilt the tin so that the mixture spreads out evenly and tap it sharply 2–3 times on the work surface to burst the air bubbles.

6 Bake in the preheated oven for 15–20 minutes until the cake springs back when touched gently and a skewer inserted into the centre comes out clean. Allow the cake to cool completely in the tin.

7 To assemble the cakes, use a 4-cm/1½-inch round cutter to cut out 16 rounds of sponge cake. Pipe buttercream on top of half the quantity of sponge rounds, then place another sponge round on top. Pipe a swirl of buttercream on the top of each cake, then adorn with decorations of your own choice, such as sugar flowers or sprinkles.

Lemon Domes with Pink Grapefruit Syrup

Fancy domed moulds shape a batch of delicate lemon sponge cakes, which are soaked in sweet grapefruit and lemon syrup after baking. They are best served in canapé spoons, or in tiny bowls along with a teaspoon so that you can scoop up the last delicious drops.

1 Preheat the oven to 180°C/350°F/Gas Mark 4. Grease 24 mini brioche moulds generously and place them on a baking sheet. Using an electric mixer, beat the butter and sugar together until light and fluffy. Gradually beat in the egg until it is well combined. Sift in the flour and baking powder, then gently fold in the lemon and grapefruit zest.

2 Divide the mixture between the prepared mini moulds, then bake in the preheated oven for about 15 minutes until golden and the cake springs back when lightly pressed. Allow the cakes to cool for 5 minutes in their moulds and then turn them out onto a wire rack to cool completely.

3 To make the syrup, use a vegetable peeler to peel strips of rind from the lemon and grapefruit. Use a small knife to remove as much pith as possible from the rinds. Tear the rinds into thin strips and then blanch them in boiling water before combining them in a saucepan with the lemon juice, grapefruit juice and sugar. Bring the syrup to the boil and continue to cook over a high heat for about 2 minutes, or until the rinds become translucent. Allow the syrup to cool before drizzling it over the cakes. If desired, sprinkle the tops of the cakes with fine strips of lemon and grapefruit zest to decorate before serving.

To make 24

60 g (2¼ oz) unsalted butter, softened, plus extra for greasing

60 g (2¼ oz) caster sugar

1 large egg

60 g (2¼ oz) self-raising flour

1 tsp baking powder

finely grated zest of 1 unwaxed lemon

finely grated zest of 1 unwaxed pink grapefruit

PINK GRAPEFRUIT SYRUP

1 unwaxed lemon

½ unwaxed pink grapefruit

5 tbsp fresh lemon juice

5 tbsp fresh pink grapefruit juice

200 g (7 oz) caster sugar

fine strips of unwaxed lemon and pink grapefruit zest, to decorate (optional)

ACTUAL SIZE

Meringues

Meringues

A meringue is an airy mixture of stiffly beaten egg whites and sugar. Most people associate meringue with light, billowy peaks atop a classic lemon meringue pie, but it can also be piped into fancy little shapes and baked to a sweet, crisp cloud to cradle delicious toppings.

Meringue Mixture

100 g (3½ oz) egg white (3 medium egg whites)
100 g (3½ oz) caster sugar
1 tsp vanilla extract
100 g (3½ oz) icing sugar, sifted

Using an electric mixer, start whisking the egg whites on a slow speed to allow small stabilizing bubbles to form, then increase the speed to high and whisk until they form soft peaks. Gradually add the caster sugar a tablespoonful at a time while whisking on a high speed until all the sugar has dissolved into the egg whites. Test a little of the meringue mixture between your fingers, and if it feels gritty, keep whisking until the mixture is smooth. Add the vanilla extract to the mixture and then slowly fold in the icing sugar using a spatula. The meringue mixture should be glossy, at which point it is ready to pipe and bake. Once you have formed your meringue into the desired shapes, bake in a very slow oven (110°C/225°F/Gas Mark ¼) until they have dried out, which will take at least an hour for smaller meringues and up to 3 hours for large pavlova nests.

TIPS

Use clean equipment when preparing the meringue mixture. Any trace of grease on mixing bowls or utensils will affect the consistency and volume of the meringue. Grease tends to cling to plastic, so if possible, mix your meringue in a glass or metal bowl.

Any trace of egg yolk will ruin your meringue. Resist the temptation to dip a finger into your bowl to get the yolk out. Some people use a piece of eggshell or a cotton-bud tip to remove the yolk, but it is often easiest just to discard that egg. For this reason, first separate your eggs into a small bowl and then add the egg whites individually to the larger mixing bowl. That way,

if some yolk slips through, you need only discard one egg white, not the whole batch.

If the sugar hasn't been allowed to dissolve and the mixture is grainy when it goes into the oven, the meringues will often leak a sugar syrup during baking.

Baking the meringues at a low temperature allows the gradual evaporation of the moisture from the mixture. If the oven is too hot, the outside of the meringue will be crunchy and browned and the centre will be chewy and sticky.

WHAT TO DO WITH ALL THE LEFTOVER EGG YOLKS?

There are lots of recipes that just call for egg yolks, so don't throw the yolks away after you have made your meringue. Here's a simple vanilla custard recipe to get you started.

Vanilla Custard

1 vanilla pod
300 ml (10 fl oz) milk
4 large egg yolks
110 g (3¾ oz) caster sugar
40 g (1½ oz) cornflour

Split the vanilla pod with a knife and place it in a saucepan. Add the milk and bring to the boil, then remove the vanilla pod and turn off the heat. Meanwhile, using an electric mixer, beat the egg yolks, sugar and cornflour together until thick and glossy. Gradually add the warm milk while continuing to beat. Pour the mixture into a saucepan and stir it over a medium heat until it boils and thickens. Cover the surface of the custard with clingfilm and allow it to cool.

Pomegranate-honey Pavlovas

Pomegranate seeds have a naturally jewel-like look and a sweet-sour taste that marries really well with the sugary meringue of a pavlova. Honey and chopped pistachios in the topping all add up to an exotically Eastern palette of flavours. You can make the meringue bases a day or two ahead of time and store them in an airtight container, adding the filling and topping just before you serve.

1 Preheat the oven to 110°C/225°F/Gas Mark ¼. Line 2 baking sheets with baking paper. Use a 4-cm/1½-inch round cutter as a guide to trace 12 evenly spaced circles on each sheet of baking paper in pencil. Turn the baking paper over so that the pencil does not rub off on the meringues while they are baking.

2 Use a palette knife to spread meringue mixture inside each circle on the baking paper. Each of these will form the base of a pavlova.

3 Spoon the remaining meringue mixture into a piping bag fitted with a small round piping tube. Pipe a border of meringue around the edge of each base. Bake the pavlovas in the preheated oven for about 1 hour, or until they have dried out. Allow the pavlovas to cool completely on the baking sheets before adding the filling.

4 In the meantime, blanch the pistachio nuts in boiling water for 10 minutes, then rub off their skins with a clean tea towel before finely crushing them. When ready to serve, stir the honey into the crème fraîche and then spoon some into each pavlova. Sprinkle with the crushed pistachio nuts and pomegranate seeds, then top with gold leaf to decorate if desired.

To make 24

1 quantity of Meringue Mixture
(*see page 27*)
50 g (1¾ oz) shelled pistachio nuts
1 tsp honey
150 g (5½ oz) crème fraîche
4 tbsp pomegranate seeds
edible gold leaf,
to decorate (optional)

ACTUAL SIZE

Micro-meringue Kisses

Light as air and not much more calorific, only their delectable fillings hold these little sugar clouds down to earth. I've given you three different flavour options to fill them: Irish coffee cream, white chocolate and pistachio cream, and delicate rose Chantilly.

To make 40

½ quantity of Meringue
Mixture (*see page 27*)

filling of your choice from the
following options
(each filling is enough to fill
all the meringues):

IRISH COFFEE CREAM

1 tbsp instant
coffee granules
1 tbsp caster sugar
2 tsp boiling water
275 ml (9 fl oz) double cream
2 tsp whisky, or to taste

ROSE CHANTILLY

200 ml (7 fl oz) whipping cream
25 g (1 oz) icing sugar, sifted
1 tsp rosewater
pink food colouring (optional)

**WHITE CHOCOLATE
& PISTACHIO CREAM**

30 g (1 oz) shelled pistachio nuts
70 g (2½ oz) white chocolate,
broken into pieces
135 ml (4½ fl oz) double cream
1 tbsp icing sugar

1 To make the Irish coffee cream filling, dissolve the coffee granules and sugar in the boiling water. Whip the cream in a bowl until it holds its shape, then stir in the coffee mixture and whisky until well incorporated.

2 To make the rose Chantilly filling, whip the cream, sugar and rosewater in a bowl until thick. If desired, tint the mixture with pink food colouring.

3 To make the white chocolate and pistachio cream filling, blanch the pistachios in boiling water for 10 minutes, then rub off their skins with a clean tea towel before finely chopping them. Melt the chocolate (*see page 41*), then allow it to cool. Lightly whip the cream with the icing sugar in a bowl, then stir in the melted chocolate and the chopped pistachio nuts.

4 Preheat the oven to 110°C/225°F/Gas Mark ¼. Line 2 baking sheets with baking paper.

5 Spoon the meringue mixture into a piping bag fitted with a small star piping tube. Pipe little rosettes about 2 cm (¾ inch) in diameter onto the lined baking sheets, then bake them in the preheated oven for about 1 hour, or until they have fully dried out. Allow the meringues to cool completely on the baking sheets before sandwiching them together with your chosen filling.

ACTUAL SIZE

Cinnamon Meringue Mushrooms

These adorable meringue mushrooms could easily be mistaken for the real thing. Don't worry about your piping skills — mushrooms grow in their own sweet way in nature and no two are alike; once the finished versions are assembled and decorated, they'll look so adorable that you won't notice the irregularities. Arrange a batch on a rustic wooden board to go with after-dinner coffee.

To make 50

1 tsp ground cinnamon

1 quantity of Meringue Mixture
(*see page 27*)

100 g (3½ oz) dark chocolate,
broken into pieces

cocoa powder,
for dusting (optional)

1 Preheat the oven to 110°C/225°F/Gas Mark ¼. Line 2 baking sheets with baking paper. Gently fold the cinnamon through the meringue mixture with a spatula. Spoon the meringue mixture into a piping bag fitted with a small round piping tube. To make the tops of the mushrooms, pipe domed rounds of meringue no more than 2.5 cm (I inch) in diameter onto one of the lined baking sheets. On the second lined baking sheet, pipe a tapered stalk for each mushroom by squeezing the piping bag to form a I cm (½ inch) round base and then slowly and evenly drawing the bag up to form a tapered stem about 2.5 cm (I inch) tall.

2 Bake the meringues in the preheated oven for about 2 hours, or until they are completely dried out. Allow them to cool completely on the baking sheets.

3 To assemble the mushrooms, use a small knife to trim the pointy end of each stalk. Melt the chocolate (*see page 41*), then use a small palette knife to spread it on the underside of each mushroom dome. Attach a stalk to each dome by placing the trimmed end of the stalk in the molten chocolate.

4 Place each mushroom, stalk side up, on a tray until the chocolate has set. If desired, dust the tops of the mushrooms with cocoa powder. Store the meringue mushrooms in an airtight container for up to 3 weeks at room temperature.

ACTUAL SIZE

Mini Dacquoise Towers

With crunchy discs of almond and hazelnut meringue alternating with a gooey mocha mousse that is very lightly set with gelatine, these minute dacquoises can really rock a cake stand for an 'occasion' tea. They're best chilled in the refrigerator for half an hour or so, then lightly dusted with cocoa powder just before serving.

1 To make the mocha mousse, first melt the chocolate (*see page 41*). In a small saucepan, bring the milk to the boil, then sprinkle over the gelatine and whisk until combined. Pour the milk into the melted chocolate and stir in the coffee granules and coffee liqueur until smooth. Set the mixture aside to cool. Whip the cream in a bowl until soft peaks form, then fold it into the chocolate mixture. Spoon the mousse into a piping bag fitted with a small petal tube and then refrigerate until required.

2 Preheat the oven to 180°C /350°F/Gas Mark 4. Line a shallow 25-cm x 38-cm (10-inch x 15-inch) baking tin with baking paper. Using an electric mixer, whisk the egg whites until soft peaks form. Gradually add the icing sugar while continuing to whisk until the mixture is firm and glossy. Gently fold in the ground hazelnuts, ground almonds and caster sugar. Spread the mixture evenly into the lined baking tin and bake in the preheated oven for about 15 minutes, or until firm to the touch. Use a 2.5-cm (1-inch) round cutter to cut out 30 rounds from the meringue while it is still warm, then allow to cool completely on a wire rack before assembling.

3 To assemble the dacquoises, pipe a ruffle border of mousse onto 10 of the meringue rounds, then place another round on top of each one. Pipe another ruffled layer of mousse onto the second round and then top with the remaining rounds. If desired, dust with cocoa powder before serving.

To make 10

6 large egg whites
75 g (2¾ oz) icing sugar,
sifted
40 g (1½ oz) ground hazelnuts
35 g (1¼ oz) ground almonds
85 g (3 oz) caster sugar
cocoa powder,
for dusting (optional)

MOCHA MOUSSE

150 g (5½ oz) dark chocolate,
broken into pieces
4 tbsp milk
2 tsp powdered gelatine
2 tsp instant coffee granules
1 tbsp coffee liqueur
200 ml (7 fl oz) double cream

ACTUAL SIZE

Mini Violet & Green Tea Macarons

No petite treat line-up would be complete without macarons. These dainty examples are small enough to have earned the soubriquet 'batchelor's buttons' – the everyday name for macarons when they were served at card-party teas in the nineteenth century. The violet and green tea flavours are subtle and unusual, and work brilliantly with a cup of smoky lapsang souchong tea.

To make 40

125 g (4½ oz) icing sugar
125 g (4½ oz) ground almonds
90 g (3¼ oz) egg whites
(3 medium egg whites)
2 tbsp water
110 g (3¾ oz) caster sugar
purple and green
food colouring
½ tsp violet
essence/flavouring
150 ml (5 fl oz) double cream
1 tsp matcha green tea powder

1 Preheat the oven to 160°C/325°F/Gas Mark 3. Line a large baking sheet with baking paper. Place the icing sugar, ground almonds and half the egg whites in a large bowl and mix to a paste.

2 Put the water and caster sugar in a small saucepan and gently stir over a low heat until the sugar has dissolved. Increase the heat and allow the mixture to boil until it thickens to a syrup. Whisk the remaining egg whites in a small bowl with a hand-held electric mixer until medium-stiff peaks form, then add the sugar syrup, whisking until the mixture becomes stiff and shiny. Stir in the almond paste. Divide the mixture between 2 bowls. Tint one bowl with purple food colouring and the other bowl with green food colouring. Add the violet essence/flavouring to the purple mixture.

3 Spoon the 2 mixtures into separate piping bags, each fitted with a small round piping tube. Pipe flat 1-cm (½-inch) rounds of meringue onto the lined baking sheet, about 2 cm (¾ inch) apart. Allow the piped rounds to stand at room temperature for 30 minutes to form a skin, then bake in the preheated oven with the door slightly ajar for 8–10 minutes until firm. Remove the macarons from the oven and allow them to cool completely on the baking sheet.

4 For the fillings, whip the cream until it holds its shape, then divide between 2 bowls. Stir the green tea powder into one bowl. Sandwich the purple macarons together with the plain whipped cream, and the green ones together with the green tea whipped cream.

ACTUAL SIZE

Chocolate

Chocolate

From its origins as a spicy drink enjoyed by Mayan Indians to its current status as a beloved confection, chocolate has always carried connotations of comfort and indulgence. The chocolate morsels in this chapter certainly punch well above their weight in sweet sophistication.

Ganache

Ganache is a mixture of melted chocolate and cream. It can be poured over bakes while still warm as a glaze or cooled and beaten to achieve a spreadable consistency. Ganache can be stored in the refrigerator for about 2 weeks, or frozen for up to 3 months. Allow the ganache to stand at room temperature to soften before use.

200 g (7 oz) dark or milk chocolate or 360 g (12½ oz) white chocolate
125 ml (4 fl oz) double cream

1 Break the chocolate into small pieces and place it in a medium bowl.

2 Bring the cream to the boil in a small saucepan over a medium heat.

3 Pour the hot cream over the chocolate and allow it to sit for 1–2 minutes before stirring it with a whisk until the mixture is smooth and all the chocolate has melted.

NOTE White chocolate can be a bit tricky to work with, as it can split (become grainy) if it is overheated. Adding more white chocolate (as compared with milk or dark chocolate) in proportion to the amount of cream will help to overcome this problem.

CHOOSING CHOCOLATE FOR BAKING

There is a huge range of eating and cooking chocolate – the difference between all the brands depends on the type of cocoa beans used, the proportion of cocoa solids and cocoa butter, the sugar content and flavourings. When buying chocolate, it is important to read the list of ingredients. Look at the percentage of cocoa solids and sugar, as this indicates the taste of the chocolate. The higher the cocoa content, the more 'chocolaty' it is going to be.

Dark chocolate with a minimum of 70 per cent cocoa solids is best for most baking recipes. You should use a chocolate that you would enjoy eating on its own.

MELTING CHOCOLATE

You don't need a double boiler (or bain-marie) to melt chocolate – you can make a double boiler by setting a heatproof bowl over a saucepan of simmering water. Make sure the base of the bowl doesn't touch the water in the saucepan. Place the chocolate, broken into pieces, in the bowl and stir until it has melted. The chocolate will be heated by the steam trapped in the saucepan. When you have finished, remove the bowl from the pan and dry the base before tipping the chocolate out, to ensure that water doesn't spill into the chocolate and spoil it.

Alternatively, you can melt chocolate in a microwave, preferably on a low (50 per cent) power setting, to avoid scorching it. Place the chocolate in a microwave-safe bowl and heat in short bursts of 30 seconds, stirring in between. How long it will take the chocolate to melt will depend on the wattage of the microwave, quantity of chocolate and even the cocoa butter content. Finish heating when most, but not all, of the chocolate is melted. Remove from the microwave and stir the chocolate constantly until it is smooth and completely melted.

MAKING CHOCOLATE DECORATIONS

Chocolate decorations can be easily made using silicone or plastic moulds. Simply pour melted chocolate into the moulds, tap them against the work surface to remove any air bubbles and then place them in the freezer. After about 10 minutes the chocolate will be set and should easily pop out when the moulds are flexed.

Gilded Caramel Shortbread Squares

Tiny squares of millionaire's shortbread are given a precious finish with a light dusting of edible gold lustre dust. Arrange them in a pyramid on the serving plate and they'll look like a little stack of gold bullion – but with the bonus that they taste delicious. If you're short of time, you can replace the cooked caramel with a layer of dulce de leche, which you can find in jars in most supermarkets.

To make about 115

250 g (9 oz) plain flour

75 g (2¾ oz) caster sugar

175 g (6 oz) unsalted butter, softened and cubed, plus extra for greasing

CARAMEL LAYER

100 g (3½ oz) unsalted butter

100 g (3½ oz) light muscovado sugar

2 x 397-g (14-oz) cans sweetened condensed milk

TOPPING

200 g (7 oz) milk chocolate, broken into pieces

edible gold lustre dust, to decorate

1 Preheat the oven to 180°C/350°F/Gas Mark 4. Lightly grease a 33-cm x 23-cm (13-inch x 9-inch) Swiss roll tin. To make the shortbread, mix the flour and sugar together in a bowl. Rub in the butter with your fingertips until the mixture resembles fine breadcrumbs. Knead the mixture together until it forms a dough, then press it evenly into the base of the prepared tin. Prick the shortbread lightly with a fork and bake in the preheated oven for about 20 minutes, or until firm to the touch and very lightly browned. Allow the shortbread to cool completely in the tin.

2 To make the caramel layer, place the butter, sugar and sweetened condensed milk in a small saucepan and gently heat until the sugar has dissolved. Bring the mixture to the boil while stirring constantly, then reduce the heat and simmer gently, stirring, for about 5 minutes, or until the mixture has thickened slightly. Pour the caramel over the shortbread and allow it to cool to room temperature.

3 For the topping, melt the chocolate (*see page 41*), then pour it over the cold caramel and leave it to set before cutting the shortbread into 2.5-cm (1-inch) squares. Use a soft paintbrush to dust the top of each square with edible gold lustre dust before serving.

ACTUAL SIZE

Chocolate Brownies with Salted Caramel Frosting

Chocolate and salted caramel is one of the classic flavour combinations, and these delectable little brownie flowers deliver a lot of taste for their delicate size. Your cooked brownie should have cooled completely before you cut the shapes out – if it's still a little warm, you'll find it hard to get clean edges on your flowers.

1 Preheat the oven to 180°C/350°F/Gas Mark 4. Line the base of a shallow 20-cm (8-inch) square baking tin with baking paper. To make the brownies, place the butter cubes and chocolate pieces in a heatproof bowl set over a small saucepan of simmering water until both have melted, stirring occasionally until mixed and smooth. Remove from the pan and allow to cool to room temperature.

2 In a separate bowl, use an electric mixer to beat the eggs and sugar together on a high speed for about 5 minutes until the mixture is thick and creamy and has doubled in volume. Pour the cooled chocolate mixture over the egg and sugar mixture, then gently fold all the ingredients together with a spatula. Sift in the flour and cocoa powder and gently combine until the mixture is a sticky, fudge-like consistency. Pour the mixture into the prepared baking tin and gently ease it into the corners with a spatula. Bake in the preheated oven for about 25 minutes, or until the top is shiny and the sides are just beginning to come away from the tin. Allow the brownie to cool completely in the tin.

3 To make the frosting, use an electric mixer to beat the butter and sugar together in a bowl for at least 5 minutes, then gradually add the dulce de leche, vanilla extract and salt while continuing to beat. Place in a piping bag fitted with a small star tube.

4 To assemble the brownies, use a small flower-shaped cutter (or another shape of your choice) to cut out 24 flower-shaped brownie bites. Pipe a zigzag of frosting on top of each brownie, then decorate each with a gold sugar flower if desired.

To make 24

185 g (6½ oz) unsalted butter, cubed

185 g (6½ oz) dark chocolate, broken into pieces

3 large eggs

275 g (9¾ oz) golden caster sugar

85 g (3 oz) plain flour

40 g (1½ oz) cocoa powder

gold sugar flowers, to decorate (optional)

SALTED CARAMEL FROSTING

160 g (5¾ oz) salted butter, softened

200 g (7 oz) icing sugar, sifted

3 tbsp dulce de leche

1 tsp vanilla extract

½ tsp salt

ACTUAL SIZE

Chocolate Cups with Mango Mousse

Crisp chocolate shells filled with a light and tangy mousse, these teeny delights are part candy, part dessert. The lime juice gives the mousse a slight citrus kick, keeping the finished treat from tasting too sweet. Use the darkest chocolate you can find to make the shells – 70 per cent cocoa solids or higher will result in the perfect trio of bitter chocolate, sharp lime and cool, fruity mango.

To make 12

150 g (5½ oz) dark chocolate, broken into pieces

5 g (⅛ oz) powdered gelatine

2 tbsp cold water

125 g (4½ oz) mango purée

1 tbsp fresh lime juice

60 g (2¼ oz) icing sugar

125 g (4½ oz) natural yogurt

250 ml (8½ fl oz) double cream, whipped until it holds its shape

fresh mint sprigs, to decorate (optional)

1 To make the chocolate cups, melt the chocolate (*see page 41*), then use a small paintbrush to paint half the melted chocolate evenly on the inside of 12 mini paper or silicone cupcake cases. Place the cases on a baking sheet and put them in the freezer until set. Use the remaining melted chocolate to paint on a second layer and then freeze the cases again until they are firm. Remove from the freezer and carefully peel away the cases to reveal the chocolate cups.

2 To make the mango mousse, soak the gelatine in the cold water in a bowl. Mix the mango purée, lime juice and icing sugar together in a saucepan over a low heat and bring to a light boil. Stir in the gelatine mixture and then remove the pan from the heat and pour the contents into a bowl. Allow the mixture to cool by placing the bowl on top of a bowl filled with ice. While the mixture is cooling, vigorously whisk it while gradually adding the yogurt. Gently fold in the whipped cream to finish.

3 Place the mango mousse in a piping bag fitted with a small star piping tube and pipe a star of mango mousse into each chocolate cup. Decorate each with a mint sprig if desired.

ACTUAL SIZE

Pistachio & White Chocolate Florentines

Sweet, sticky and crunchy all at once, Florentines make the perfect teatime treat. These miniature versions stand out flavour-wise with an unusual combination of cranberries and pistachios, rather than the customary cherries and almonds or hazelnuts. If you keep the proportions the same, you can experiment with your own fruit and nut combinations to put your stamp on the recipe.

1 Preheat the oven to 180°C/350°F/Gas Mark 4. Line the base of a 23-cm x 33-cm (9-inch x 13-inch) baking sheet with baking paper. Melt the butter together with the sugar in a saucepan over a low heat. Use a spoon to beat in the flour, cream and lemon juice. Chop the pistachio nuts and dried cranberries, then stir them into the mixture with the flaked almonds.

2 Spread the Florentine mixture evenly onto the lined baking sheet and then bake in the preheated oven for about 15 minutes until golden but not brown. Remove the baking sheet from the oven and quickly use a 2.5-cm (1-inch) round cutter to cut out 30 rounds from the Florentine bake while it is still hot. Allow the rounds to cool completely on a clean, lined baking sheet.

3 Melt the chocolate (see page 41), then dip the backs of the cooled Florentines in the melted chocolate to coat and place, chocolate side down, on the lined baking sheet. Transfer the baking sheet to the refrigerator for about 20 minutes until the chocolate has set. Drizzle the remaining melted chocolate over the tops of the Florentines and return to the refrigerator for a further 10 minutes until set before serving.

TIP You can also bake the Florentine mixture in the holes of silicone mini muffin baking tins.

To make 30

40 g (1½ oz) unsalted butter

50 g (1¾ oz) caster sugar

1 tbsp plain flour

1 tbsp double cream

1 tsp fresh lemon juice

50 g (1¾ oz) shelled pistachio nuts, skins removed (*see page 29*)

40 g (1½ oz) dried cranberries

50 g (1¾ oz) flaked almonds

100 g (3½ oz) white chocolate, broken into pieces

ACTUAL SIZE

Pastry

Pastry

There are many different types of pastry, but if you only want to turn to one kind, then probably the most useful and versatile pastry is shortcrust, which has both a sweet and savoury version, making it ideal for creating a whole range of mini bites to suit different tastes.

Shortcrust Pastry (pâte brisée)

Shortcrust pastry is made using a 'half-fat-to-flour' ratio. Fat (such as butter) is rubbed into plain flour to create a loose mixture that is then bound together with a small amount of iced water. If you don't want to get your fingers dirty, it can also be made with a food processor. For both methods, once the pastry is made, wrap it in clingfilm and chill in the refrigerator for 10–15 minutes before using.

125 g (4½ oz) plain flour
pinch of salt
55 g (2 oz) unsalted butter, cubed
2–3 tbsp iced water

METHOD 1 (BY HAND)

Place the flour and salt in a large bowl and add the cubes of butter.

Use your fingertips to rub the butter into the flour until the mixture resembles coarse breadcrumbs with no large lumps of butter remaining. Lift the mixture up as you rub the butter in so that the air going through it keeps it cool. Shake the bowl intermittently to bring the lumps of butter to the surface. Work quickly so that the mixture does not become greasy.

Stir in just enough of the iced water to bind the pastry together.

METHOD 2 (FOOD PROCESSOR)

Alternatively, put the flour, salt and butter in a food processor and pulse until the fat is rubbed into the flour. With the motor running, gradually add the iced water through the feed tube until the pastry comes together. Add just enough water to bind it and then stop.

Sweet Shortcrust Pastry (pâte sucrée)

This rich, sweet pastry makes a delicious base for tarts or fruit pies.

90 g (3¼ oz) unsalted butter, softened
60 g (2¼ oz) caster sugar
3 large egg yolks
200 g (7 oz) plain flour, plus extra for dusting

Beat the butter and sugar together in a bowl until light and fluffy, then beat in the egg yolks one at a time until fully incorporated.

Mix in the flour until the mixture comes together as a ball of dough. Tip the pastry out onto a floured work surface and knead briefly until smooth. Wrap in clingfilm and chill in the refrigerator for at least an hour. Alternatively, the pastry can be frozen for use at a later date.

FREEZING PASTRY

Wrap the pastry tightly in clingfilm, place in a freezer-safe bag and freeze for up to 2 months. Thaw the pastry in the refrigerator for 3–4 hours before rolling and shaping. Fully baked unfilled pastry cases can be stored in an airtight container at room temperature for up to 3 days.

BAKING PASTRY

Common practice with tartlets is to line and fill the pastry cases with ceramic beans or rice before baking to prevent the pastry from shrinking and puffing up. You can eliminate this step by putting the unbaked pastry cases in the freezer for 15 minutes to set the pastry and prevent it from shrinking during baking. You can also prick the base of the pastry cases with a fork before baking to help maintain their shape.

Mini Mille-Feuilles with Elderflower Cream

Confected from the lightest puff pastry (in French, *millefeuille* means 'thousand leaves'), thin slices of strawberry and cream infused with the understated but heady flavour of elderflower, these diminutive pastries look elegant and taste like the essence of a sunny summer's day.

To make 24

375 g (13 oz) ready-rolled puff pastry, just thawed if frozen

1 tbsp elderflower syrup

2 tsp caster sugar

125 ml (4 fl oz) double cream

10 fresh strawberries, hulled and thinly sliced

icing sugar, for dusting

1 Preheat the oven to 200°C/400°F/Gas Mark 6. Line a large baking sheet with baking paper. Cut the puff pastry sheet into small rectangles 5 cm (2 inches) long and 2.5 cm (1 inch) wide. Arrange on the lined baking sheet and use a fork to prick holes into the surface of each one. Place a sheet of baking paper over the top of the pastries.

2 Place another baking sheet on top of the pastries (to stop the pastry from rising too much during baking), then bake in the preheated oven for 10–15 minutes until golden. Allow the puff pastry layers to cool completely on the baking sheet.

3 Mix the elderflower syrup and caster sugar into the cream in a bowl and then whisk until thick. To assemble each mille-feuille, spread the cream over a pastry layer, then top with strawberries and another layer of pastry. Spread more cream on top of the second pastry layer, then top with strawberries and a final pastry layer. Dust the top of each mille-feuille with icing sugar before serving.

TIP The puff pastry layers can be baked ahead of time and stored in an airtight container.

ACTUAL SIZE

Heart-shaped Vol au Vents with Raspberry Coulis

Literally French for 'windblown', conveying just how light they are, vol au vents are more usually found with savoury fillings – but this sweet, nutty, chocolaty version ticks all the flavour boxes, and the heart shape adds an extra cute touch. A drizzle of raspberry coulis added just before serving will make them look as delicious as they taste.

1 To make the raspberry coulis, place the raspberries, sugar and lemon juice in a frying pan and heat until the raspberries start to break down. Transfer the mixture to a food processor and blend until smooth. Pass through a fine sieve to remove the pips, then set aside until ready to serve.

2 Preheat the oven to 180°C/350°F/Gas Mark 4. Line 2 or 3 baking sheets with baking paper. Lay the puff pastry sheet on a floured work surface and use a small heart cutter, no more than 4 cm (1½ inches) at its widest point, to cut out 80 heart shapes. Use a slightly smaller heart cutter to cut a small heart out of the centre of half the quantity of hearts – these will be the heart rings. Use a fork to prick holes in the plain hearts. Brush eggwash around the edge of the plain hearts, then place the heart rings on top of the plain hearts. Be careful to ensure that the eggwash does not drip down the sides, otherwise the pastry will not rise. Place the hearts on the lined baking sheets, then place them in the freezer for 5 minutes, or until firm.

3 Brush the tops of the hearts with eggwash before baking them in the preheated oven for 12 minutes, or until golden brown. Allow them to cool completely on the baking sheets.

4 Use a spoon to gently remove the centre of each vol au vent, then fill with the chocolate ganache. If desired, decorate with the finely chopped roasted hazelnuts and a light dusting of cocoa powder, then serve with a drizzle of the raspberry coulis.

TIP Reserve the puff pastry trimmings for using in other recipes, such as the palmiers on page 58 or the cheese straws on page 124.

To make 40

375 g (13 oz) ready-rolled puff pastry, just thawed if frozen

plain flour, for dusting

eggwash (1 large egg beaten with 1 tbsp cold water)

1 quantity of Dark Chocolate Ganache
(*see page 41*)

50 g (1¾ oz) roasted blanched hazelnuts, finely chopped, to decorate (optional)

cocoa powder, for dusting (optional)

RASPBERRY COULIS

250 g (9 oz) raspberries, fresh or frozen

1 tbsp icing sugar

juice of ½ lemon

ACTUAL SIZE

Chai-spiced Palmiers

Indian-inspired chai spicing is becoming more and more popular in cappuccinos and lattes, but it's still uncommon as a flavouring for cakes or cookies. But the moreish mix of cinnamon, ginger, cardamom and cloves is pressed into service here as a filling for the crisp pastries known colloquially as elephant's ears. Kitten's ears, perhaps, in this miniature form?

To make 50

115 g (4 oz) caster sugar, plus extra (optional) for sprinkling

½ tbsp ground cinnamon

½ tsp ground ginger

½ tsp ground cloves

½ tsp ground cardamom

190 g (6½ oz) ready-rolled puff pastry, just thawed if frozen

35 g (1¼ oz) butter, melted and cooled

1 Mix the sugar with the cinnamon, ginger, cloves and cardamom in a bowl. Unwrap the puff pastry and lay it on a clean work surface. Sprinkle the chai sugar mixture over the pastry then roll a non-stick rolling pin over the top of the pastry to help the chai sugar stick to it.

2 Cut the pastry into strips 7.5 cm (3 inches) wide. Tightly roll both sides of each pastry strip inwards so that they meet in the middle. Wrap the rolled logs in clingfilm and chill in the refrigerator for about 30 minutes, or until firm. Meanwhile, preheat the oven to 200°C/400°F/Gas Mark 6. Line 2 baking sheets with baking paper.

3 Slice the firm pastry logs into thin slices with a serrated knife and place the slices, evenly spaced and cut side up, on the lined baking sheets. Brush each palmier with melted butter and sprinkle with extra sugar, if desired. Bake in the preheated oven for 5 minutes, or until caramelized and brown, then turn over with a spatula and bake for a further 3–5 minutes until caramelized on the other side. Transfer to a wire rack to cool.

TIP This is a great recipe for using up leftover bits of puff pastry.

ACTUAL SIZE

Baked Raspberry Tartlets

Crisp, sweet pâte sucrée is used to make these tartlet cases, which are then finished with a brown butter filling and topped off with a fresh raspberry. Brown butter lends the tartlets a tasty, slightly 'nutty' flavour; having used it once, you'll probably find lots of other applications for it when you bake.

To make 36

1 quantity of Sweet Shortcrust
Pastry (*see page 53*)
icing sugar, for dusting

BROWN BUTTER FILLING

115 g (4 oz) unsalted butter,
plus extra for greasing
100 g (3½ oz) caster sugar
2 large eggs
1 tsp vanilla extract
pinch of salt
35 g (1¼ oz) plain flour,
plus extra for dusting
75 g (2¾ oz) raspberries,
fresh or frozen

1 Grease individual mini tartlet tins – those used here measured 4 cm (1½ inches) in length (you can prepare and bake the tartlets in batches according to how many tins you may have). Roll out the pastry on a lightly floured work surface to about 5 mm (¼ inch) thick. If using almond-shaped mini tartlet tins like those here, use a rectangular cutter to cut out rectangles of pastry that are wider and longer than the tins. Drape the pastry into the prepared tartlet tins, gently pushing the pastry into the bottom edges and against the tin sides to make strong pastry cases. Press down firmly along the rims of the tins to cut off the excess pastry. Use a fork to prick holes all over the bases and sides of the tartlet cases. Place on a baking sheet, then place in the freezer for at least 30 minutes to firm up. In the meantime, preheat the oven to 180°C/350°F/Gas Mark 4.

2 Bake the tartlet cases in the preheated oven for 7–8 minutes until they are lightly golden.

3 To make the filling, melt the butter in a small saucepan over a low heat, then increase the heat to medium and cook it until there are brown flecks on the base of the pan. The butter will foam up and then settle back down again while browning and will produce a nutty aroma. Remove from the heat.

4 Beat the sugar, eggs, vanilla extract and salt together in a bowl with a whisk. Whisk in the flour gently, then pour in the browned butter in a steady stream while whisking constantly. Place a raspberry in each tartlet case, then pour over the filling until it almost fills the case. Return to the oven for a further 10 minutes until golden brown and the filling is set. Allow the tartlets to cool completely in the tins before removing and serving with a dusting of icing sugar.

ACTUAL SIZE

Lemon-Lime Gems

The combination of crisp, sweet shortcrust pastry and sharp home-made lemon and lime curd ensure these morsels are gobbled up quickly whatever the occasion. The tartlet cases can be baked ahead of time and frozen – if you have a jar of lemon-lime curd to hand, you'll never be more than 20 minutes away from a batch of zingy gems.

1 To make the lemon-lime curd, whisk the lemon juice, lime juice, sugar and eggs together in a medium heatproof bowl. Add the butter, then set the bowl over a small saucepan of simmering water. Cook the curd, while stirring often, for at least 8 minutes, or until it thickens and coats the back of a spoon. Remove from the pan, allow to cool, stirring occasionally, then cover with clingfilm and store the curd in the refrigerator until required.

2 Grease individual mini tartlet tins – those used here measured 2.5 cm (1 inch) in diameter (you can prepare and bake the tartlets in batches according to how many tins you may have). Roll out the pastry on a lightly floured work surface to about 5 mm (¼ inch) thick. Use a 5-cm (2-inch) round cutter to cut out rounds of pastry. Drape the pastry rounds into the prepared tartlet tins, gently pushing the pastry into the bottom edges and against the tin sides to make strong pastry cases. Press down firmly along the rims of the tins to cut off the excess pastry. Use a fork to prick holes all over the bases and sides of the tartlet cases. Place on a baking sheet, then place in the freezer for at least 30 minutes to firm up. In the meantime, preheat the oven to 180°C/350°F/Gas Mark 4.

3 Bake the tartlet cases in the preheated oven for 7–8 minutes until golden brown. Allow to cool completely in the tins, then remove and divide the lemon-lime curd between them.

To make 48

1 quantity of Sweet Shortcrust Pastry
(*see page 53*)
plain flour, for dusting

LEMON-LIME CURD

4 tbsp fresh lemon juice
4 tbsp fresh lime juice
55 g (2 oz) caster sugar
4 large eggs, at room temperature
100 g (3½ oz) unsalted butter, chopped

ACTUAL SIZE

Chocolate Ganache-filled Tartlets

Rich chocolate pastry is baked in tiny fluted tartlet tins, then filled with a white chocolate ganache and decorated with melted chocolate. You can pre-bake the cases several hours ahead, but don't store them in the refrigerator, or the pastry will lose its crispness.

To make 24

85 g (3 oz) plain flour,
plus extra for dusting

2 tbsp cocoa powder

60 g (2¼ oz) unsalted butter,
softened and cubed,
plus extra for greasing

2 tbsp golden caster sugar

1 large egg yolk

FILLING & DECORATION

1 quantity of warm White
Chocolate Ganache
(*see page 41*)

100 g (3½ oz) milk chocolate,
melted (*see page 41; optional*)

1 To make the pastry, sift the flour and cocoa powder into a large mixing bowl, then rub in the butter with your fingertips until the mixture resembles fine breadcrumbs. Mix in the sugar and egg yolk to form a soft dough. If the mixture is too dry, add a little cold water. Wrap the pastry in clingfilm and chill it in the refrigerator for an hour.

2 Preheat the oven to 180°C/350°F/Gas Mark 4. Grease individual mini tartlet tins – those used here measured 4 cm (1½ inches) square (you can prepare and bake the tartlets in batches according to how many tins you may have). Roll out the pastry on a lightly floured work surface to about 5 mm (¼ inch) thick. Use a small knife to cut out 24 squares slightly larger than your mini tartlet tins. Drape the pastry squares into the prepared tins, gently pushing the pastry into the bottom edges and against the tin sides to make strong pastry cases. Press down firmly along the rims of the tins to cut off the excess pastry. Use a fork to prick holes all over the bases and sides of the tartlet cases. Place on a baking sheet, then place in the freezer for at least 30 minutes to firm up.

3 Bake the tartlet cases in the preheated oven for 8–10 minutes until crisp. Allow to cool in the tins, then remove and fill each one with the white chocolate ganache. Allow them to set at room temperature for several hours. If desired, fill a small piping bag fitted with a small round piping tube with the melted milk chocolate and pipe flourishes on the tartlets to decorate. Allow to set before serving.

ACTUAL SIZE

Choux

Choux

Choux pastry is a light, twice-cooked pastry made with plain flour, butter, water and eggs. It is most commonly used to make profiteroles, éclairs and choux puffs – here scaled down to diminutive form – but it serves equally well for savoury pastries.

Choux Pastry
(pâte à choux)

60 g (2¼ oz) unsalted butter
175 ml (6 fl oz) water
105 g (3¾ oz) plain flour
3 large eggs, lightly beaten

Combine the butter with the water in a medium saucepan and bring the mixture to the boil. Add the flour, all at once, and beat with a wooden spoon over a medium heat until the mixture forms a smooth ball. Transfer the mixture to a small bowl and beat in the eggs, one at a time, with a hand-held electric mixer until the mixture becomes smooth and glossy. The choux pastry is now ready to pipe and bake.

Note: When making choux pastry, it is important to be sure that each egg is fully incorporated into the batter before adding the next. Don't worry if the batter separates and looks curdled at first. Keep beating, and it will come together nicely.

BAKING CHOUX PASTRY

Choux pastry needs a hot oven, so it is important to preheat the oven and make sure it has come up to temperature before baking the choux pastries.

Bake the choux pastries one sheet at a time. Choux pastry rises when the water held in the pastry turns to steam in the heat of the oven, so too many sheets in the oven at one time will create too much humidity and your choux pastries won't be able to dry out and will be soggy and collapse. The additional batches will sit and wait quite happily for their turn in the oven.

Resist the temptation to peek inside the oven during the baking time. Opening the door will release heat from the oven, which will affect how much the pastries puff up. Choux pastries will be golden brown in colour when they are completely baked.

Choux pastries are generally slit with a knife during or after baking to allow steam to escape from the inside. After releasing the steam, return the pastries to the oven for a few minutes to dry out before filling.

Choux pastry tastes best on the day it is made, but this is not always practical. Instead, the pastry can be made the day before, left in a covered bowl and refrigerated overnight. You can then pipe and bake the pastry the following day. Alternatively, unfilled cooked choux pastries such as éclairs and profiteroles can be frozen in plastic containers. When you are ready to use them, thaw the frozen pastries on baking sheets and put them into a hot oven for 5 minutes, or leave them out in their containers to thaw at room temperature for an hour or so.

FILLING CHOUX PASTRY

Most fillings will start to soften the pastry once they have been piped inside. Choux pastries should therefore ideally be eaten within a couple of hours of filling.

SAVOURY TREATS

Crisp choux pastry is very versatile and delicious in savoury recipes. To boost the flavour when making savoury dishes, add a little salt and pepper or some grated cheese or spices to the choux pastry dough before baking it.

Cute Croquembouches

The classic *croquembouche* – literally 'something that crunches in the mouth' – is a tower of crisp profiteroles, filled with crème patissière and drizzled with toffee, which is often served at a wedding or first communion. These minute versions, stuck together with vanilla custard and spun toffee, take a little time to put together, but would add a festive touch to a special tea party – and they're tiny, so no need to share!

To make 20

½ quantity of Choux Pastry
(*see page 69*)
½ quantity of Vanilla Custard
(*see page 27*)

TOFFEE

115 g (4 oz) caster sugar
65 ml (2¼ fl oz) water

1 Preheat the oven to 220°C/425°F/Gas Mark 7. Line 2–3 baking sheets with baking paper. Spoon the choux pastry into a piping bag fitted with a 5-mm (¼-inch) round piping tube. Pipe 320 tiny balls of pastry about 1 cm (½ inch) apart onto the lined baking sheets. Use a damp pastry brush to smooth the top of each ball if they have peaks before baking them in the preheated oven for 7 minutes. Reduce the oven temperature to 180°C/350°F/Gas Mark 4, then bake for a further 5 minutes, or until the choux balls are crisp. Allow to cool completely on the baking sheets.

2 To make the toffee, combine the sugar and water in a small saucepan and stir over a medium heat without boiling until the sugar has dissolved. Bring the sugar mixture to the boil and allow it to simmer, uncovered and without stirring, until the mixture is golden. Remove the pan from the heat and allow the toffee to stand for a few minutes until any bubbles subside.

3 Dip one side of 7 choux balls into the custard, then arrange them in a tight circle about 4 cm (1½ inches) in diameter; the custard will help stick them together. Dip the base of another 5 choux balls into the custard, then arrange them in a circle on top of the other choux balls. Dip the base of 4 more choux balls into the custard, then arrange on top of the choux balls to complete the cone shape. Spin the toffee around the cone to secure all the choux balls in place. Make up the other *croquembouches* in the same way.

ACTUAL SIZE

Feathered Chocolate Éclairs

Éclairs were originally named *pain à la duchesse* and these versions, miniaturized and with neatly feathered glazed tops, are certainly treats fit for any modern lady of fashion. Choux is one of the more forgiving pastries to cook with, provided that you remember to cut the puffs to release the steam inside as soon as you take them out of the oven.

To make 50

1 quantity of Choux Pastry
(*see page 69*)
300 ml (10 fl oz) double cream
½ tsp vanilla extract

CHOCOLATE GLAZE

25 g (1 oz) unsalted butter,
cubed
100 g (3½ oz) dark chocolate,
broken into pieces
90 g (3¼ oz) icing sugar, sifted
100 ml (3½ fl oz) boiling water

WHITE FONDANT ICING
(OPTIONAL, FOR FEATHERED
ICING PATTERN)

3 tsp fondant icing sugar, mixed with
1 drop of water

1 Preheat the oven to 200°C/400°F/Gas Mark 6. Line 2–3 baking sheets with baking paper. Spoon the choux pastry into a piping bag fitted with a 5-mm (¼-inch) round piping tube. Pipe 50 small, thin lines of choux pastry about 4 cm (1½ inches) long, evenly spaced apart, onto the lined baking sheets. Use a damp pastry brush to smooth the top of each line of choux pastry before baking them in the preheated oven for 10 minutes. Cut a small horizontal slit at the end of each éclair to allow the steam to escape, then return them to the oven for a further 5 minutes. Allow to cool completely on a wire rack.

2 Whip the cream in a bowl until it holds its shape, then stir in the vanilla extract. Fill a piping bag fitted with a small round piping tube with the cream. Insert the tube into the slit in each éclair and gently squeeze the piping bag so that the cream fills the cavity. A little bit of cream will come back out of the slit if the éclair has been completely filled.

3 To make the chocolate glaze, stir the butter, chocolate and sugar together in a heatproof bowl set over a small saucepan of simmering water until the mixture is glossy and smooth. Gradually stir in the boiling water until the mixture loosens and reaches the consistency of thick cream. Use a small palette knife to spread the glaze over the top of each éclair. If desired, pipe thin lines of white fondant icing into the wet chocolate glaze across the width of the éclair, and drag a cocktail stick from one end of the éclair to the other to create a feathered pattern.

ACTUAL SIZE

Rose Religieuses

Practise your piping skills before undertaking a batch of these flowery little religieuses, so called because the original chocolate-glazed, cream-piped versions were thought to look like nuns in their black and white habits. They're not hard to make, but you need to be neat. I opted for a dazzling fuchsia glaze on my rose-flavoured minis, but you could pick a paler pink if you prefer a more subtle effect.

1 Preheat the oven to 200°C/400°F/Gas Mark 6. Line 2–3 baking sheets with baking paper. Spoon the choux pastry into a piping bag fitted with a 5-mm (¼-inch) round piping tube. Pipe 24 balls about 2.5 cm (1 inch) in diameter and 24 smaller balls about 1 cm (½ inch) in diameter onto the lined baking sheets. Bake in the preheated oven for 10–12 minutes. Cut a small horizontal slit at the bottom of each ball to allow the steam to escape, then return them to the oven for a further 5 minutes. Allow to cool completely on a wire rack.

2 To make the crème patissière, bring the milk and vanilla extract to the boil in a small saucepan, then simmer for a few minutes. Allow the mixture to cool. Beat the egg yolks and sugar together in a large bowl with a hand-held electric mixer or whisk until they are pale, then beat in the flour and cornflour. Pour the milk into the mixture while whisking constantly. Transfer the mixture to the saucepan and then gently bring it to the boil while whisking constantly. Turn off the heat, then pour the mixture into a clean bowl, cover with clingfilm and allow to cool. Chill for several hours or overnight before use.

3 To make the rose fondant icing, add the rosewater and fuchsia food colouring to the fondant icing sugar in a bowl and mix with a spoon until smooth. The icing will be thick and have the consistency of thick cream.

4 To fill the choux buns, place the crème patissière in a piping bag fitted with a small round piping tube. Insert the tube into the slit in each choux bun and gently squeeze the piping bag so that the crème patissière fills the cavity. A little bit of crème patissière will come back out of the slit if the choux bun has been completely filled.

5 Spread fondant icing on the top of the choux buns using a small palette knife and then stick the small choux buns on top of the larger ones while the icing is still wet. If desired, place a small edible pearl or silver ball on top of each religieuse.

6 Fit a piping bag with a small star piping tube and fill with the buttercream. Pipe lines of buttercream up from the base of the top choux bun to the fondant icing. Refrigerate until ready to serve. The religieuses will keep in the refrigerator for up to 2 days.

To make 24

1 quantity of Choux Pastry
(*see page 69*)
⅓ quantity of Vanilla Buttercream
(*see page 13*)
small edible pearls or silver balls,
to decorate (optional)

CRÈME PATISSIÈRE

225 ml (8 fl oz) milk
1 tsp vanilla extract
3 large egg yolks
100 g (3½ oz) caster sugar
15 g (½ oz) plain flour
15 g (½ oz) cornflour

ROSE FONDANT ICING

½ tsp rosewater
fuchsia pink food colouring
200 g (7 oz) fondant icing sugar

ACTUAL SIZE

Caramel-amaretto Paris-Brest Miniatures

Invented in 1891 to commemorate the Paris-Brest cycle race, the classic recipe for these choux rings usually flavours them with coffee. The petits fours-scaled pastries shown here have an almondy amaretto-crème filling instead and a sticky caramel glaze on top. Small sugar pearls add some shimmer to the end result.

To make 30

1 quantity of Choux Pastry
(*see page 69*)
edible pearls, to decorate
(optional)

AMARETTO CRÈME FILLING

150 ml (5 fl oz) double cream
1 tbsp amaretto, or to taste

CARAMEL GLAZE

50 g (1¾ oz) unsalted butter
60 g (2¼ oz) soft dark brown sugar
2 tbsp glucose syrup
2 tbsp milk
125 g (4½ oz) icing sugar, sifted

1 Preheat the oven to 200°C/400°F/Gas Mark 6. Line 2–3 baking sheets with baking paper. Spoon the choux pastry into a piping bag fitted with a 5-mm (¼-inch) round piping tube. Pipe 30 rings about 4 cm (1½ inches) in diameter, evenly spaced apart, onto the lined baking sheets. Use a damp pastry brush to smooth the top of each ring before baking them in the preheated oven for 10 minutes. Cut a small horizontal slit in each ring to allow the steam to escape, then return them to the oven for a further 5 minutes. Slice each ring horizontally in half and then allow to cool completely on a wire rack.

2 To make the amaretto crème filling, whip the cream to stiff peaks in a bowl with a hand-held electric mixer, then gently stir in the amaretto with a spoon. Place the cream in a piping bag fitted with a small star piping tube and pipe small dots of cream between the ring halves.

3 To make the caramel glaze, heat the butter, brown sugar and glucose syrup in a small saucepan over a medium heat, stirring, until the butter and sugar have melted and the mixture begins to boil. Whisk in the milk, and then add the icing sugar. Continue to whisk the mixture until it is smooth and thickened. Remove the caramel from the heat and allow it to cool. Use a palette knife to spread the caramel glaze over the top of the rings. If desired, sprinkle edible pearls over the caramel glaze before it has set.

ACTUAL SIZE

Biscuits

Biscuits

Always delicious, home-made biscuits
in mini-morsel form are even more
appealing, and are easy to dress up
for a special occasion. They are also
relatively robust, making packaging
and transporting worry free.

Vanilla Sugar Cookies

Having a recipe on hand for a biscuit without a raising agent is useful if you need to make tiny biscuits. These vanilla sugar biscuits hold their shape when baking.

Makes 45

175 g (6 oz) unsalted butter, softened
200 g (7 oz) caster sugar
2 eggs
1 tsp vanilla extract
400 g (14 oz) plain flour, plus extra for dusting

Using an electric mixer, beat the butter and sugar together until light and creamy. Gradually beat in the eggs one at a time, followed by the vanilla extract.

Sift in the flour and mix gently with a spoon until well combined. Form the dough into a flattened disc, wrap it in clingfilm and chill in the refrigerator for at least an hour until firm.

Preheat the oven to 180°C/350°F/Gas Mark 4. Line a baking sheet with baking paper. Allow the dough to soften slightly at room temperature, then roll it out on a lightly floured work surface. Use cutters to cut out your desired shapes, then place them on the lined baking sheet. Bake the biscuits in the preheated oven for 10–12 minutes until the edges start to turn gold. Allow to cool completely on a wire rack before decorating.

TIPS

Chilling before baking helps softer doughs keep their shape and makes them easier to work with. The chilling time given is the optimum time for easy rolling and shaping. To speed up chilling, wrap the dough in clingfilm and place in the freezer. About 20 minutes of chilling in the freezer is equal to one hour in the refrigerator.

Biscuits should be baked on flat baking sheets lined with baking paper, or on a silicone mat. The baking sheet can have slightly raised edges, but biscuits will not brown evenly if it is too deep.

A baking sheet should be cool or at room temperature when dough is placed on it, otherwise the dough will start to melt, which will affect the shape and texture of the biscuit.

Ensure that all the biscuits on one baking sheet are of a uniform thickness and size so they will bake in the same amount of time.

Allow biscuits to cool before storing them; if they are still warm, they will 'sweat' and go soggy.

FREEZING BISCUIT DOUGH

Most unbaked biscuit doughs freeze extremely well and can be kept frozen for up to 4–6 weeks. The most important thing to bear in mind is that the dough will absorb any odours present in your freezer if it's not properly wrapped and sealed, so double-wrap it securely in clingfilm. When you are ready to bake, simply allow the dough to thaw in the refrigerator. This will take several hours, so plan ahead.

FREEZING BAKED BISCUITS

Freezing baked, un-iced biscuits is a great way to preserve their freshness; they will keep in the freezer for up to 3–4 weeks. Double-wrap securely in clingfilm. When ready to eat them, just let them come to room temperature, or pop them in the microwave on high for about 30 seconds. (Times will differ depending on the size of biscuit you are thawing.) Once thawed, the biscuits can be iced or decorated.

Coffee Bean Biscuits

Fragrant coffee shortbread is shaped into tiny oval biscuits that look exactly like lightly roasted coffee beans, and aren't a lot bigger – the characteristic line down the middle of each 'bean' is marked using a cocktail stick. Pop a handful into the saucer of each guest's cup of Java so that they can alternately crunch and sip.

To make 200

175 g (6 oz) unsalted butter, softened

200 g (7 oz) caster sugar

2 eggs

2 tsp espresso powder or instant coffee granules

2 tbsp boiling water

½ tsp vanilla extract

400 g (14 oz) plain flour

1 Using an electric mixer, beat the butter and sugar together until light and creamy. Gradually beat in the eggs one at a time until well combined. Mix the espresso powder or coffee granules with the boiling water to form a syrup. Add the coffee syrup and vanilla extract to the butter and sugar mixture and beat until smooth.

2 Sift in the flour, then mix gently with a spoon until well combined. Form the dough into a flattened disc, wrap it in clingfilm and chill in the refrigerator for at least an hour until firm.

3 Preheat the oven to 180°C/350°F/Gas Mark 4. Line 2 baking sheets with baking paper. Allow the dough to soften slightly at room temperature. Roll small ovals of the biscuit dough about 1 cm (½ inch) long and place them on the lined baking sheets. Press a cocktail stick horizontally along each biscuit to imprint a line down the centre to form the coffee bean shape. Bake the biscuits in the preheated oven for 3–5 minutes until just firm to the touch. Allow them to cool completely on a wire rack.

ACTUAL SIZE

Frosted Jewel Biscuits

These little gems are topped with a royal icing that sets quite hard, so they're a good choice if you need a treat that you can transport; they'll arrive looking neat and crisp. And with a range of different hues of pastel icing, they make an exceptionally pretty plateful – perfect for everything from a reading-group coffee break to a kids' party favour.

To make 75

250 g (9 oz) plain flour, plus extra for dusting

½ tsp salt

½ tsp baking powder

2 tbsp caster sugar

90 g (3¼ oz) unsalted butter, softened and cubed

140 ml (4½ fl oz) milk

ROYAL ICING

250 g (9 oz) icing sugar, sifted

1 large egg white

½ tsp fresh lemon juice

assorted food colourings, such as pink, purple, orange, green

1 Mix all the dry ingredients together in a large bowl and then rub the butter into the mixture with your fingertips until it resembles coarse breadcrumbs. Gradually mix in the milk with a spoon to bind the crumbs together and form a dough. Wrap the dough in clingfilm and chill in the refrigerator for at least an hour until firm.

2 Preheat the oven to 180°C/350°F/Gas Mark 4. Line a large baking sheet with baking paper. Roll out the dough on a lightly floured work surface, then use a 2-cm (¾-inch) round cutter to cut out rounds. Place them on the lined baking sheet and bake in the preheated oven for 20 minutes, or until they are lightly golden in colour. Allow the biscuits to cool completely on a wire rack before decorating.

3 To make the royal icing, use an electric mixer to mix the icing sugar and egg white together on a low speed for about 5 minutes until the icing has a stiff-peak consistency. Mix in the lemon juice with a wooden spoon. Divide the icing into several bowls and add a small amount of a different food colouring to each one to create a variety of colours. Use a piping bag fitted with a small star piping tube to pipe a small rosette of coloured royal icing onto each biscuit. Allow the icing to dry at room temperature (preferably overnight) before serving.

ACTUAL SIZE

Strawberry Sandwich Biscuits

Crisp sugar biscuits with a fruity filling; if you have any home-made strawberry preserve, it will elevate these into the luxury league, but even if you use a good-quality shop-bought version, they will still taste lovely. If you don't have a miniature cutter to make the hole in the centre of the top biscuit, you can use the end of a drinking straw.

1 Using an electric mixer, beat the butter and sugar together until light and creamy. Gradually beat in the eggs one at a time until well combined, followed by the vanilla extract.

2 Sift in the flour and mix gently with a spoon until well combined. Form the dough into a flattened disc, wrap it in clingfilm and chill in the refrigerator for at least an hour until firm.

3 Preheat the oven to 180°C/350°F/Gas Mark 4. Line a baking sheet with baking paper. Allow the dough to soften slightly at room temperature. Roll out the dough on a lightly floured work surface to about 5 mm (¼ inch) thick. Use a 3.5-cm (1⅜-inch) round cutter to cut out rounds and place them on the lined baking sheet. Use a small star cutter (or another shape if desired) to cut out a hole from the centre in every second biscuit. Bake the biscuits in the preheated oven for 10–12 minutes until the edges are lightly browned and the biscuits are just firm to the touch. Allow the biscuits to cool completely on a wire rack.

4 Spread strawberry preserve on each solid biscuit, then press a biscuit with a hole in it on top. If desired, dust with icing sugar before serving.

To make 40

175 g (6 oz) unsalted butter, softened

200 g (7 oz) caster sugar

2 large eggs

½ tsp vanilla extract

400 g (14 oz) plain flour, plus extra for dusting

6 tbsp strawberry preserve

icing sugar, for dusting (optional)

ACTUAL SIZE

Tiered Biscuit Towers

The brown sugar and cocoa powder in the biscuit dough give these masterpieces a rich chocolaty edge, while the stacked construction makes them look like miniature wedding cakes, topped off with icing beads and pretty sugar roses. If you wanted to make them for an actual wedding, they could serve as elegant placecard props for the table settings, or as pretty favours for the guests.

To make 24

225 g (8 oz) unsalted butter, softened

225 g (8 oz) soft light brown sugar

1 large egg, beaten

425 g (15 oz) plain flour, plus extra for dusting

30 g (1 oz) cocoa powder

sugar roses or other edible decorations, to decorate

ROYAL ICING

250 g (9 oz) icing sugar, sifted

1 large egg white

½ tsp fresh lemon juice

1 Using an electric mixer, beat the butter and sugar together until light and creamy. Gradually beat in the egg until well combined.

2 Sift in the flour and cocoa powder and mix on a slow speed until the ingredients start to clump together into a ball. Wrap the dough in clingfilm and chill in the refrigerator for at least an hour until firm.

3 Preheat the oven to 180°C/350°F/Gas Mark 4. Line 2 baking sheets with baking paper. Allow the dough to soften slightly at room temperature, then roll it out on a lightly floured work surface until 5 mm (¼ inch) thick.

4 Use 2.5-cm (1-inch), 3.5-cm (1⅜-inch) and 4-cm (1½-inch) round cutters to cut out 3 different-sized rounds for each biscuit. Place on the lined baking sheets and bake in the preheated oven for 10–12 minutes until they are lightly browned and just firm to the touch. Allow to cool completely on a wire rack.

5 To make the royal icing, use an electric mixer to mix the icing sugar and egg white together on a low speed for about 5 minutes until the icing has a stiff-peak consistency. Mix in the lemon juice with a wooden spoon. Use a small amount of royal icing to assemble each biscuit tower with the smallest biscuit on the top tier and the largest on the bottom tier so that the tower resembles a miniature 3-tiered cake. Fill a piping bag fitted with a 5-mm (¼-inch) round piping tube with the remaining royal icing and pipe small dots around the rim of each tier of each biscuit tower. Top the towers with a sugar rose or another edible decoration, using royal icing to secure the decoration in place. Allow the royal icing to dry at room temperature (preferably overnight) before serving.

ACTUAL SIZE

Coconut Noughts & Crosses

This chewy coconutty mixture is simple to shape into anything you like – here they've been formed into miniature noughts and crosses (play a game and winner eats all...), but you could just as easily make stars, flowers, butterflies or any other simple shape. They're the quickest treats in the book to make, but they're baked at a very low heat, so they take a little extra time in the oven to cook.

1 Preheat the oven to 140°C/275°F/Gas Mark 1. Line a baking sheet with baking paper. Whisk the egg whites in a clean, grease-free bowl until they form stiff peaks. Gently fold in the sugar and desiccated coconut with a spatula until evenly combined. If desired, divide the mixture into separate bowls and colour the mixture with different food colourings.

2 Allow the mixture to stand for 15–20 minutes to firm up before shaping it into small noughts and crosses. The mixture can be shaped by hand, or it can be pressed inside small cutters (for this project I used an 'O' and an 'X' cutter from an alphabet set). Place the macaroons on the lined baking sheet and bake in the preheated oven for 45 minutes, or until they just start to turn golden in colour. Allow the macaroons to cool completely on a wire rack before serving.

TIP Bear in mind that the colour of the macaroons, and any other tinted biscuit dough, may darken when baked.

To make 30

2 large egg whites
150 g (5½ oz) caster sugar
150 g (5½ oz) unsweetened
desiccated coconut
assorted food colourings,
such as pink and purple
(optional)

ACTUAL SIZE

Polka-dot Lemon Shortbreads

Zesty lemon shortbread is topped with spotted icing, and each biscuit is finished with a ribbon – these petites are almost (but not quite) too pretty to eat. The technique of 'flooding' icing to add extra details is a useful one to have up your sleeve, especially for themed biscuits; you can create any design you like to suit the occasion.

To make 45

175 g (6 oz) unsalted butter, softened

200 g (7 oz) caster sugar

2 large eggs

½ tsp vanilla extract

1 tsp limoncello or fresh lemon juice

400 g (14 oz) plain flour, plus extra for dusting

finely grated zest of ½ unwaxed lemon

ROYAL ICING

250 g (9 oz) icing sugar, sifted

1 large egg white

½ tsp limoncello or fresh lemon juice

yellow food colouring

1 Using an electric mixer, beat the butter and sugar together until light and creamy. Gradually beat in the eggs one at a time, followed by the vanilla extract and limoncello or lemon juice.

2 Sift in the flour and add the lemon zest, then mix gently with a spoon until well combined. Form the dough into a flattened disc, wrap it in clingfilm and chill in the refrigerator for at least an hour until firm.

3 Preheat the oven to 180°C/350°F/Gas Mark 4. Line a baking sheet with baking paper. Allow the dough to soften slightly at room temperature, then roll it out on a lightly floured work surface until 5 mm (¼ inch) thick. Use a 4-cm (1½-inch) round cutter to cut out rounds. Place the rounds on the lined baking sheet and then use the end of a round piping tube to cut out a little hole in the side of each biscuit. Bake in the preheated oven for 10–12 minutes until the edges start to turn gold. Allow the biscuits to cool completely on a wire rack.

4 To make the royal icing, use an electric mixer to mix the icing sugar and egg white together on a low speed for about 5 minutes until the icing has a stiff-peak consistency. Mix in the limoncello or lemon juice with a wooden spoon. Fill a piping bag fitted with a small round piping tube with one-third of the royal icing. Pipe around the edge of each biscuit and around the edge of the small hole in each biscuit. Spoon half the remaining icing into a bowl and colour it with yellow food colouring. Slowly stir a few drops of water into the icing until it is a runny consistency. Add a few drops of water to the remaining white icing until it is also a runny consistency. Fill 2 squeeze bottles with the icings. Gently squeeze the white icing into the outlined section of each biscuit to 'flood' it until the icing covers all of the surface. While the icing is still wet, squeeze small drops of the yellow icing onto the surface to create a polka-dot pattern. Allow the biscuits to dry at room temperature (preferably overnight), then tie a thin ribbon bow through each hole.

TIP Leave the biscuits to dry under a lamp to achieve a shiny surface.

ACTUAL SIZE

Cupcakes

Cupcakes

There are oodles of cupcake recipes in books and online, but it's harder to find as many recipes for their miniature friends. Fortunately, it is not difficult to downsize your favourite cupcake recipes with a few simple tips.

MAKING MINI CUPCAKES

Most cupcake recipes can be used to make mini cupcakes. Mini cupcake baking tins hold roughly one-third of the amount of regular cupcake baking tins, so if you have a recipe that yields 12 full-sized cupcakes, you'll get about 36 minis from the same amount of mixture. It is much easier to start with the full recipe and make a big batch of miniature cupcakes than to reduce the quantities of the ingredients in the recipe.

Once you have made your cupcake mixture, line the mini cupcake tin holes with mini cupcake cases and add mixture to each one until they are two-thirds full. It is often quite tricky and time-consuming to use a teaspoon to scoop the mixture into the cases, so to save time, fill a large disposable piping bag fitted with a small round piping tube with the cupcake mixture and pipe the mixture into the cases. Piping the mixture will also help to ensure that the cupcakes are approximately the same size.

BAKING TIMES FOR MINI CUPCAKES

While most regular cupcakes take about 20–25 minutes to bake, miniature cupcakes bake in a shorter period of time, and on average only need 10–15 minutes until they are done. After 10 minutes of baking time, it is useful to insert a skewer into one of the cupcakes to see if they are baked all the way through. If the skewer doesn't come out clean when withdrawn from the cupcake, return the cupcakes to the oven for a few more minutes.

It's easy to over-bake miniature cupcakes, so be sure to keep a close eye on them while they are baking in the oven.

ADDING INGREDIENTS TO MINI CUPCAKES

If your regular cupcake recipe calls for ingredients such as fruit, nuts or chocolate chips to be stirred into the mixture, it is important to be mindful that unless these ingredients are chopped finely, they can overwhelm the miniature cupcakes. While whole blueberries are a nice surprise in a regular-sized cupcake, they can take up most of the space in a mini cupcake case, leaving little room for the mixture. Remember to always scale down your extra ingredients so that they are proportional to the size of the miniature cupcakes.

DECORATING MINI CUPCAKES

It is also very easy to make a miniature cupcake look too top heavy. Decorating with small toppings works best, such as sprinkles, crushed nuts and small chocolates, instead of whole fruit or large fondant toppers.

If you intend to display your cupcakes on a cake stand or on a plate, it is easiest to pipe frosting on top of them and add any other decorations once the display has been arranged. Reducing the amount of times you need to pick up and move the cupcakes will help to ensure that the frosting is not smudged. Cupcakes should be frosted on the day they are to be served.

STORING CUPCAKES

Cupcakes can be stored overnight in a cupcake box at room temperature. Cupcakes with perishable frostings should ideally be eaten the same day, or refrigerated and consumed the following day. Undecorated cupcakes can be frozen after baking. Bring them to room temperature when you're ready to decorate them.

Peanut Butter Chocolate Cupcakes

Every treat list needs a chocolate cupcake, and this is mine – dark chocolate and brown sugar combine to give the mix a great flavour, while ground almonds keep the sponge light and moist. The cakes are finished with rosettes of peanut butter frosting – a natural pairing with the rich cake, and one that balances the chocolate beautifully.

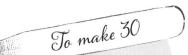

To make 30

60 g (2¼ oz) dark chocolate, chopped

160 ml (5½ fl oz) water

90 g (3¼ oz) unsalted butter, softened

225 g (8 oz) soft dark brown sugar

2 large eggs

100 g (3½ oz) self-raising flour

2 tbsp cocoa powder

40 g (1½ oz) almond flour

PEANUT BUTTER FROSTING

50 g (1¾ oz) unsalted butter, softened

100 g (3½ oz) smooth peanut butter

300 g (10½ oz) golden icing sugar, sifted

50 ml (2 fl oz) milk

2 tbsp salted roasted peanuts

1 Preheat the oven to 180°C/350°F/Gas Mark 4. Line 30 holes of mini cupcake baking tins with mini cupcake cases. To make the cupcakes, stir the chocolate and water together in a small saucepan over a low heat until smooth. Using an electric mixer, beat the butter, sugar and eggs together until light and fluffy. Stir the flour, cocoa powder, almond flour and warm chocolate into the mixture until well combined.

2 Spoon the mixture into the cupcake cases until they are half full and bake in the preheated oven for about 15 minutes, or until a skewer inserted into the centre of a cupcake comes out clean. Allow the cupcakes to cool for a few minutes in the tin before turning them onto a wire rack to cool completely.

3 For the peanut butter frosting, use an electric mixer to beat the butter and peanut butter together on a high speed for about 2 minutes until light and fluffy, then gradually beat in the sugar and milk until light and smooth. Fill a piping bag fitted with a small star piping tube with the frosting and pipe a small rosette of frosting onto each cupcake. Top with half a peanut to finish.

ACTUAL SIZE

White Russian Cupcakes

Based on the classic cocktail that's traditionally made with vodka, coffee liqueur and cream, these innocent-looking minis are much less potent but just as delicious as the drink that inspired them. If you want an alcohol-free version, though, replace the coffee liqueur and vodka with a little coffee flavouring – your cupcakes will taste just as good.

To make 24

125 g (4½ oz) plain flour
½ tsp baking powder
¼ tsp bicarbonate of soda
small pinch of salt
5 tbsp Kahlúa, or to taste
2 tsp instant coffee granules
110 g (4 oz) unsalted butter,
softened
175 g (6 oz) caster sugar
2 large egg whites
5 tbsp semi-skimmed milk
small sugar flowers, to decorate
(optional)

WHITE CHOCOLATE
VODKA GANACHE

150 ml (5 fl oz) double cream
30 g (1 oz) unsalted butter
250 g (9 oz) white chocolate,
melted (see page 41)
6 tbsp vodka

KAHLÚA SWISS MERINGUE
BUTTERCREAM

120 g (4¼ oz) caster sugar
2 large egg whites
250 g (9 oz) unsalted butter, softened
6 tbsp Kahlúa, or to taste

1 Preheat the oven to 180°C/350°F/Gas Mark 4. Line a 24-hole mini muffin baking tin with mini cupcake cases. Mix the flour, baking powder, bicarbonate of soda and salt together in a bowl and set aside. In a separate bowl, whisk together the Kahlúa and coffee granules. Using an electric mixer, beat the butter and sugar together until light and fluffy. Add the egg whites one at a time and mix until well combined. Alternate adding the milk, flour mixture and Kahlúa mixture to the cake mixture and beat until combined.

2 Spoon the cake mixture into the cupcake cases until they are two-thirds full, then bake in the preheated oven for about 12 minutes, or until a skewer inserted into the centre of a cupcake comes out clean. Turn the cupcakes onto a wire rack to cool completely before filling and decorating.

3 While the cupcakes are baking, make the ganache. Heat the cream and butter in a small saucepan until small bubbles appear, then remove the pan from the heat and add the melted white chocolate. Stir until completely combined and smooth, then stir in the vodka. Cover with clingfilm and chill the ganache in the refrigerator for about an hour.

4 For the buttercream, add the sugar to the egg whites in a heatproof bowl set over a small saucepan of simmering water and whisk until the sugar dissolves completely. Remove the bowl from the pan and use an electric mixer to whisk the mixture on a high speed for about 5 minutes until it is bright white in colour and does not move in the bowl. Divide the butter into 8 blocks. Reduce the mixer speed to medium and add the butter one block at a time, then mix in the Kahlúa. Place the buttercream in a piping bag fitted with a small star piping tube.

5 Use a small knife or a cupcake corer to remove the top two-thirds of the core from the centre of each cupcake, then fill with the ganache. Pipe a buttercream swirl on top of each cupcake and, if desired, add a small sugar flower to finish.

ACTUAL SIZE

Mojito Cupcakes

The pleasure of a great mojito lies in the balance of its flavours; rum, lime and mint all need to be in harmony for the drink to taste good. These mini mojitos are all you could wish for in a cocktail — in a cupcake. Once baked, the little cakes are soaked in a rum and mint syrup before being topped with a swirl of lime buttercream frosting, with a touch more rum. Intoxicating, delicious and the perfect mini-dessert for a special dinner.

1 Preheat the oven to 180°C/350°F/Gas Mark 4. Line 2 x 24-hole mini cupcake baking tins with mini cupcake cases. To make the cupcakes, mix the flour, baking powder, bicarbonate of soda and salt together in a bowl and set aside. In a separate bowl, whisk together the buttermilk, rum and vanilla extract. Using an electric mixer, beat the butter and sugar together for about 5 minutes until light and fluffy. Add the eggs one at a time and mix until well combined. Alternate adding the flour mixture and buttermilk mixture to the cake mixture and beat until combined.

2 Spoon the mixture into the cupcake cases until they are two-thirds full, then bake in the preheated oven for 12–15 minutes, or until a skewer inserted into the centre of a cupcake comes out clean. Turn the cupcakes onto a wire rack to cool for a few minutes.

3 While the cupcakes are baking and cooling slightly, make the rum syrup. Place the butter, sugar and water in a saucepan and bring to the boil, stirring often until the butter has completely melted and the sugar has dissolved. Remove the pan from the heat and carefully add the rum; the mixture will bubble, so take care not to burn yourself. Add the lime zest and juice and mint, then allow the syrup to infuse for 5 minutes. Remove the mint leaves.

4 Use a skewer or cocktail stick to poke holes all over the tops of the warm cupcakes, then immediately spoon over the rum syrup and allow them to soak it up. Leave the cupcakes to cool completely before frosting them.

5 For the buttercream, use an electric mixer to beat the butter on a high speed for about 2 minutes until light and fluffy, then gradually beat in the sugar (about 200 g/7 oz at a time) on a low speed. Once all the sugar is incorporated, increase the speed to high again and mix for another 2–3 minutes. Add the rum and lime juice and mix on a medium speed until well incorporated. Place the buttercream in a piping bag fitted with a small star piping tube and pipe a swirl onto each cupcake. Sprinkle lime zest on top to finish.

ACTUAL SIZE

To make 48

375 g (13 oz) plain flour

1 tsp baking powder

½ tsp bicarbonate of soda

pinch of salt

275 ml (9 fl oz) buttermilk

1 tbsp dark rum

½ tsp vanilla extract

225 g (8 oz) unsalted butter, softened

450 g (1 lb) caster sugar

4 medium eggs

RUM SYRUP

55 g (2 oz) unsalted butter

225 g (8 oz) caster sugar

4 tbsp cold water

4 tbsp dark rum

finely grated zest and juice of ½ unwaxed lime

25 g (1 oz) fresh mint leaves

LIME & RUM BUTTERCREAM

250 g (9 oz) unsalted butter, softened

600 g (1 lb 5oz) icing sugar, sifted

4 tbsp dark rum

juice of 1 unwaxed lime, and finely grated zest, to decorate

White Chocolate Mudcakes

Mudcakes are usually made with dark chocolate, but these little cupcakes are the vanilla versions, flavoured with creamy white chocolate and topped off with a two-tone swirl of raspberry-vanilla buttercream and sugar heart confetti – making them perfect little treats for Valentine's Day or an anniversary.

To make 48

125 g (4½ oz) unsalted butter, softened and chopped

85 g (3 oz) white chocolate

225 g (8 oz) caster sugar

125 ml (4 fl oz) milk

75 g (2¾ oz) plain flour

75 g (2¾ oz) self-raising flour

1 large egg

sprinkles, such as mini pink hearts, to decorate

BUTTERCREAM

175 g (6 oz) unsalted butter, softened

350 g (12 oz) icing sugar, sifted

1 tsp vanilla extract

2 tbsp cooled boiled water

2 tbsp raspberry preserve

1 Preheat the oven to 180°C/350°F/Gas Mark 4. Line 2 x 24-hole mini cupcake baking tins with mini cupcake cases. Stir the butter, white chocolate, sugar and milk together in a small saucepan over a low heat until smooth. Transfer to a medium bowl and allow to cool to room temperature.

2 Whisk the flours into the cooled mixture, then whisk in the egg. Spoon the mixture into the cupcake cases until they are two-thirds full, then bake in the preheated oven for about 15 minutes, or until a skewer inserted into the centre of a cupcake comes out clean. Allow the cupcakes to cool for a few minutes in the tin before turning them onto a wire rack to cool completely.

3 To make the buttercream, use an electric mixer to beat the butter and icing sugar together on a high speed for about 5 minutes until light and fluffy. Add the vanilla extract and the water, then mix on a medium speed until well incorporated. Divide the mixture between 2 bowls. Stir the raspberry preserve through one bowl of buttercream and leave the other bowl plain. Fill one side of a piping bag fitted with a small star piping tube with the vanilla buttercream and the other side with the raspberry buttercream. Squeeze the buttercream out of the bag and into a bowl until you achieve a 2-toned effect. Pipe a 2-toned swirl of buttercream onto each cupcake, and scatter with sprinkles, such as mini pink sugar hearts, to finish.

TIP Add any sprinkles or decorations while the buttercream is still fresh otherwise they won't stick in place.

ACTUAL SIZE

Coconut Cupcakes

These little layered beauties will charm anyone nostalgic for the childish pleasure of coconut ice. A fluffy vanilla interior is given a strawberry and whipped cream filling, frosted with a pink glacé icing and, as a final touch, rolled in desiccated coconut – a wonderful range of flavours squeezed into a bite-sized cupcake.

To make 36

150 g (5½ oz) self-raising flour

90 g (3¼ oz) unsalted butter, softened

1 tsp vanilla extract

115 g (4 oz) caster sugar

2 large eggs

2 tbsp milk

GLACÉ ICING & TOPPING

115 g (4 oz) icing sugar

½ tsp unsalted butter

2 drops of pink food colouring

1 tbsp hot water

75 g (2¾ oz) sweetened desiccated coconut

10 tbsp strawberry preserve

300 ml (10 fl oz) double cream, whipped until it holds its shape

sugar flowers, to decorate (optional)

1 Preheat the oven to 180°C/350°F/Gas Mark 4. Line 36 holes of mini cupcake baking tins with mini cupcake cases. Sift the flour into a bowl, then add the butter, vanilla extract, sugar, eggs and milk. Using an electric mixer, beat the ingredients together on a low speed until well combined. Increase the mixing speed to medium, then beat until the mixture becomes pale.

2 Spoon the cake mixture into the cupcake cases until they are half full, then bake in the preheated oven for about 12 minutes, or until a skewer inserted into the centre of a cupcake comes out clean. Turn the cupcakes onto a wire rack to cool completely.

3 To make the glacé icing, sift the sugar into a small heatproof bowl and stir in the butter, pink food colouring and hot water to make a thick paste. Place the bowl over a small saucepan of simmering water and stir until the icing reaches a spreadable consistency.

4 Once the cupcakes have cooled, use a palette knife to spread the glacé icing on the top of each cupcake, then immediately dip them into the desiccated coconut. Allow the icing to set for a few minutes, then use a small knife to carefully cut a hole in the top of each cupcake. Fill each hole two-thirds full with strawberry preserve. Place the whipped cream in a piping bag fitted with a small star piping tube and pipe a swirl of cream on top of each preserve-filled hole. If desired, add a sugar flower on top to finish.

ACTUAL SIZE

Savoury

Savoury

Cute bakes don't have to be limited to desserts. They say the best things come in small packages, and it's no exception when it comes to flavour-packed, bite-sized canapés. Traditionally, canapés have a base made from puff pastry or biscuit, which can support any number or combination of toppings.

Puff Pastry

Making puff pastry takes time and physical effort, so the recipes in this book recommend that you use shop-bought puff pastry. However, if time is on your side and you fancy making your own puff pastry, here's a recipe you can try:

250 g (9 oz) plain flour, plus extra for dusting
½ tsp salt
40 g (1½ oz) unsalted butter, chilled and cubed
125 ml (4 fl oz) iced water
210 g (7½ oz) unsalted butter, softened

Place the flour and salt in a large bowl and add the cubes of chilled butter.

Use your fingertips to rub the butter into the flour until the mixture resembles fine breadcrumbs. Make a well in the centre of the mixture and pour in the iced water. Mix the ingredients together until well combined. Form the mixture into a ball, wrap it in clingfilm and chill in the refrigerator for 30 minutes.

Use a lightly floured rolling pin to roll out the pastry into a 10-cm x 30-cm (4-inch x 12-inch) rectangle. Place the softened butter between 2 sheets of clingfilm and tap with a rolling pin to make a 8-cm x 9-cm (3¼-inch x 3½-inch) rectangle. Lay the pastry on a lightly floured work surface with a short edge closest to you. Remove the clingfilm from the butter and place it in the centre of the pastry. Fold the end close st to you over the butter, then fold the opposite end over the top so that the butter is enclosed in the pastry.

Turn the pastry 90 degrees clockwise and gently press the edges together. Use a lightly floured non-stick rolling pin to gently tap the pastry to flatten the butter. Roll out the pastry to a 10-cm x 30-cm (4-inch x 12-inch) rectangle and repeat the folding process as before. Cover the pastry with clingfilm and place in the refrigerator for 30 minutes to rest.

Remove the pastry from the refrigerator and repeat the rolling and folding process 2 more times. Cover with clingfilm and place in the refrigerator for 30 minutes to rest. Repeat the rolling and folding process a further 2 times and then place in the refrigerator for 30 minutes to rest. (The dough should have been folded and rolled 6 times altogether.)

Remove the pastry from the refrigerator, unwrap and give it a final 2 rolls and folds before rolling it out to the size required for your chosen recipe.

TIPS

Canapés should be no bigger than one bite or else you are risking entering the realm of finger food.

Fresh, in-season ingredients will always lead you to the most beautiful tasting canapés.

Often canapés need building at the last minute, so have all the components ready in advance to make assembly quick and easy. It's also a good idea to have a clear vision of what the finished canapés will look like well in advance so that you can quickly plate them up and serve them once the guests arrive, rather than fiddling about with finishing touches.

Spinach & Feta Triangles

Inspired by the Greek *spanakopita* but encased in puff pastry rather than the more traditional filo, these walnut-sized snacks are airy and light, with a crunchy outside and a cheesy spinach filling warmed with a hint of nutmeg. Served warm, they're the perfect finger food, which means they'll disappear very quickly, so consider baking a double batch.

To make 40

250 g (9 oz) baby spinach
leaves, chopped

2 spring onions, thinly sliced

100 g (3½ oz) feta cheese,
coarsely chopped

finely grated zest of ½ unwaxed lemon

¼ tsp ground nutmeg

30-cm x 19-cm (12-inch x 7½-inch)
piece of ready-rolled puff pastry,
just thawed if frozen

plain flour, for dusting

1 medium egg, beaten

salt and freshly ground
black pepper

1 Preheat the oven to 200°C/400°F/Gas Mark 6. Line 2 baking sheets with baking paper. Bring a saucepan of salted water to the boil, add the spinach and spring onions and blanch for 1 minute. Drain well, squeezing out any excess water, and place in a bowl. Add the feta, lemon zest and nutmeg, season to taste with salt and pepper and mix well.

2 Lay the puff pastry on a floured work surface and use a 4-cm (1½-inch) square cutter to cut out 40 squares. Divide the filling between the pastry squares, then brush the edges with the beaten egg. Fold the pastry in half diagonally to enclose the filling and make a triangle. Pinch the edges to seal.

3 Place the triangles on the lined baking sheets, then brush the tops with beaten egg. Bake in the preheated oven for 15 minutes, or until puffed and golden. Serve warm.

ACTUAL SIZE

Caesar Salad Bites

The American classic makes a good party snack when it's reduced to miniature form. Garlic butter-infused bread is baked until golden to make a croûton-like tart to contain finely shredded lettuce, crispy bacon morsels and Parmesan cheese. Quails' egg halves complete the picture. Pretty to look at and gorgeous to eat.

To make 24

butter, for greasing

10 slices of white bread

100 g (3½ oz) garlic butter
(or plain butter if you prefer),
melted

1 tbsp vegetable or olive oil

3 bacon rashers,
cut into thin slices

12 quails' eggs

1 Little Gem lettuce

25 g (1 oz) Parmesan cheese,
finely grated

CAESAR SALAD
DRESSING

1 garlic clove

2 anchovy fillets in oil,
drained

5 tbsp mayonnaise

1 tbsp white wine vinegar

grating of Parmesan cheese

salt and freshly ground
black pepper

1 Preheat the oven to 160°C/325°F/Gas Mark 3. Grease the holes of a 24-hole mini muffin baking tin. Remove the crusts from the slices of bread. Use a 4-cm (1½-inch) round cutter to cut out rounds from the bread, then brush them with the melted garlic butter and press into the greased holes of the baking tin. Bake in the preheated oven for 10 minutes, or until they are golden. Heat the oil in a frying pan and fry the bacon slices until crispy. Place them on kitchen paper to drain and cool.

2 To make the Caesar salad dressing, peel the garlic clove and crush it finely using a garlic crusher into a small bowl. Add the anchovies and use a fork to mash them to a paste on the side of the bowl. Add the mayonnaise, vinegar and Parmesan cheese, and stir it all together. Season to taste with salt and pepper. If the dressing is too thick, thin it down with a few teaspoons of water.

3 To softly boil the quails' eggs, place them in a saucepan and cover with cold water. Bring to the boil, then immediately remove from the heat. Cool the eggs under cold running water, then carefully peel and cut in half.

4 To assemble the salads, finely shred the lettuce and top with the Caesar salad dressing. Fill the bread tartlet cases with the lettuce, then add a little Parmesan cheese and a sprinkling of crispy bacon pieces. Place a quails' egg half on the top of each salad to finish.

ACTUAL SIZE

Pesto Pinwheels

Pinwheels, redolent of paper windmill toys and spinning fireworks, instantly create a festive feel. These spicy pastry versions are super-fast to put together – the different ingredients can be bought ready-made, and with some neat-fingered assembly, you're only half an hour away from a sophisticated-looking canapé.

1 Preheat the oven to 180°C/350°F/Gas Mark 4. Line a baking sheet with baking paper. Roll out the puff pastry on a floured work surface until about 2 mm (¹⁄₁₆ inch) thick. Use a 4-cm (1½-inch) square cutter to cut out squares of pastry. For each square, use a small knife to make a cut diagonally from each corner of the square to 1 cm (½ inch) from the centre to create 4 segments. Lightly brush the edge of each segment with milk.

2 Spoon a small dollop of pesto into the centre of each square and then, starting at the top right-hand corner, work clockwise around the square folding one corner of each segment towards the centre to conceal the pesto and create the pinwheel shape.

3 Place the tomato purée in a piping bag fitted with a small round piping tube. Brush the surface of the pastry with milk, then pipe a small dot of tomato purée in the centre of each pinwheel. Sprinkle dried oregano over the pinwheels and place them on the lined baking sheet, then bake them in the preheated oven for about 10 minutes, or until they are golden brown and crisp. Serve them warm or cold.

To make 50

200-g (7-oz) block of puff pastry,
thawed if frozen

plain flour, for dusting

2 tbsp milk

4 tbsp pesto

5 tbsp tomato purée

dried oregano, for sprinkling

ACTUAL SIZE

Mini Blini Stacks with Smoked Salmon

Blinis are Russian pancakes, traditionally made with buckwheat and served with caviar. My versions are a little lighter (I used plain flour) and much more purse-friendly (smoked salmon replaces the caviar), but they taste just as good. The blinis should be cool before you assemble the stacks, making them a very versatile canapé base.

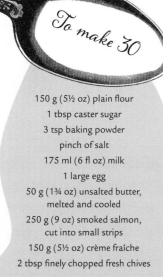

To make 30

150 g (5½ oz) plain flour

1 tbsp caster sugar

3 tsp baking powder

pinch of salt

175 ml (6 fl oz) milk

1 large egg

50 g (1¾ oz) unsalted butter, melted and cooled

250 g (9 oz) smoked salmon, cut into small strips

150 g (5½ oz) crème fraîche

2 tbsp finely chopped fresh chives

1 Sift the flour, sugar, baking powder and salt into a large bowl. Gradually whisk in the milk and egg, then half the melted butter. Cover and chill the mixture in the refrigerator for 30 minutes. When the mixture is ready to use, spoon it into a squeeze bottle.*

2 Heat a large frying pan over a medium-high heat and lightly brush the pan with a little of the remaining butter. Squeeze small rounds, about 2.5 cm (1 inch) in diameter, of the blini mixture into the pan. Cook for about 30 seconds, or until browned lightly underneath and bubbles begin to appear on the surface. Use a spatula to gently turn the blinis over, then cook the other side for a further 30 seconds until brown. Repeat with the remaining blini mixture to create at least 90 mini blinis.

3 To serve, stack 3 blinis on top of each other, with the smoked salmon and some of the crème fraîche sandwiched in between the bottom 2 layers. Top each stack with the remaining crème fraîche and a sprinkling of chives. Keep the blini stacks refrigerated until ready to serve.

***NOTE** A squeeze bottle will help control the size of the blinis, as it will allow the mixture to be gradually squeezed into the frying pan until the desired size is reached. If you don't have a squeeze bottle, just use a teaspoon to transfer the mixture to the pan.

ACTUAL SIZE

Caramelized Onion Galettes with Goat's Cheese

Take your time softening the onion for these little puff pastry galettes – helped along by the wine and brown sugar, they'll take on a delicious savoury-sweet flavour that's beautifully offset by the tangy goat's cheese and a few thyme leaves, carefully picked so there are no rogue pieces of stalk to spoil the texture.

To make 45

1 tbsp olive oil

1 brown onion, thinly sliced

1 tbsp soft light brown sugar

5 tbsp red wine

375 g (13 oz) ready-rolled puff pastry, just thawed if frozen

plain flour, for dusting

eggwash (1 large egg beaten with 1 tbsp cold water)

75 g (2¾ oz) goat's cheese, cut into small slices

3 tsp fresh thyme leaves, plus extra sprigs (optional) to garnish

salt and freshly ground black pepper

1 Preheat the oven to 180°C/350°F/Gas Mark 4. Line 2 baking sheets with baking paper. Heat the oil in a pan and fry the onion over a low heat until softened. Add the sugar and cook for a further 5 minutes. Add the red wine and salt and pepper to taste and simmer the onion, stirring regularly, for about 5 minutes until sticky and caramelized.

2 Place the puff pastry sheet on a floured work surface and use a 3-cm (1¼-inch) round cutter to cut out 45 rounds of pastry. Use a smaller round cutter, about 2.5-cm (1-inch) in diameter, to score a circle inside each pastry round to create a small rim. Place the rounds, evenly spaced, on the lined baking sheets. Brush the rim of each pastry round lightly with eggwash, then bake in the preheated oven for 10 minutes.

3 Remove the galettes from the oven and use the back of a teaspoon to press down the inner rounds so that they drop down, or come away. Fill each pastry case with the caramelized onion, then top with a small slice of goat's cheese. Scatter the thyme leaves over the galettes, then return them to the oven to bake for a further 10 minutes. If desired, add extra thyme sprigs on top to garnish before serving warm or cold.

ACTUAL SIZE

Profiteroles with Blue Cheese Mousse

Although you may have a mental picture of profiteroles smothered in sweet chocolate sauce, the savoury version tastes terrific, too. A rich, chive-dotted blue cheese filling is piped into the choux puffs to create the ultimate cocktail party canapé.

To make 60

½ quantity of Choux Pastry
(*see page 69*)

BLUE CHEESE MOUSSE

175 g (6 oz) soft blue cheese
115 g (4 oz) cream cheese
5 tbsp double cream
½ bunch of fresh chives,
finely chopped, plus extra
for sprinkling (optional)
salt and freshly ground
black pepper

1 Preheat the oven to 220°C/425°F/Gas Mark 7. Line 2 baking sheets with baking paper. Spoon the choux pastry into a piping bag fitted with a 5-mm (¼-inch) round piping tube. Pipe 60 small balls of the pastry about 2 cm (¾ inch) in diameter, evenly spaced, onto the lined baking sheets. Use a damp pastry brush to smooth the top of each ball if they have peaks before baking them in the preheated oven for 10 minutes. Reduce the oven temperature to 180°C/350°F/Gas Mark 4, then bake for a further 5 minutes, or until the choux balls are crisp. Make a small slit in the base of each ball to release the steam, then allow to cool completely on the baking sheets.

2 To make the blue cheese mousse, blend the blue cheese and cream cheese together in a food processor or in a bowl with a hand-held electric mixer until completely smooth. Season to taste with salt and pepper. In a separate bowl, whip the cream until soft peaks form. Fold the whipped cream into the blue cheese mixture and stir until the mixture is creamy, then fold in the finely chopped chives.

3 To fill the profiteroles, transfer the mousse into a piping bag fitted with a 2.5-mm (⅛-inch) round piping tube. Insert the tube into the slit in the bottom of the profiterole and gently squeeze the piping bag so that the mousse fills the cavity of the profiterole. A little bit of mousse will come back out of the hole if the profiterole has been completely filled. Repeat until all the profiteroles are filled. Serve scattered with a sprinkling of chives, if desired.

ACTUAL SIZE

Cheese-straw Bundles with Paprika

Tiny bundles of cheese straws laced with paprika for a hint of smoky heat, then tied together with fresh chives – this is a great use for leftover puff pastry. And mildly fiddly chive-tying apart, these are quick to make, too. Serve with a glass of something sparkling.

To make 50 bundles

200-g (7-oz) block of puff pastry, thawed if frozen

plain flour, for dusting

100 g (3½ oz) Gruyère cheese, finely grated

1 tbsp sweet smoked paprika

1 small egg, beaten

2 tbsp freshly grated Parmesan cheese

1 bunch of fresh chives

1 Roll out the puff pastry on a floured work surface until about 1.5 cm (⅝ inch) thick. Scatter one-third of the Gruyère cheese and one-third of the smoked paprika evenly over the surface of the pastry, then use a non-stick rolling pin to roll the ingredients firmly into the pastry.

2 Fold the pastry in half and roll it out again until about 1.5 cm (⅝ inch) thick. Repeat the process twice more with the remaining thirds of the Gruyère and paprika, then roll out the pastry into a 28-cm x 18-cm (11-inch x 7-inch) rectangle about 2 mm (1/16 inch) thick. Brush the pastry with the beaten egg and sprinkle over the Parmesan cheese. Allow the pastry to rest in the refrigerator for 30 minutes. Meanwhile, preheat the oven to 180°C/350°F/Gas Mark 4. Line a large baking sheet with baking paper.

3 Cut the pastry into tiny strips about 4 cm (1½ inches) long and 3 mm (⅛ inch) wide. Carefully take each strip of pastry and twist each end in opposite directions until the whole strip is evenly twisted, then lay them on the lined baking sheet. Bake the cheese straws in the preheated oven for about 5 minutes, or until they are golden brown and crisp. Allow them to cool completely on the baking sheet.

4 To serve, group 4–5 of the cheese straws together into small bundles and tie them together with the chives.

ACTUAL SIZE

Index

About the author

Fiona started cake decorating and food styling as a hobby in 2009 when she moved to London from Sydney. Inspired by the vintage era, she started her blog Icing Bliss (www.icingbliss.blogspot.com), where she records her adventures baking and trawling through car boot sales collecting vintage treasures. She also posts online tutorials to show readers how to make vintage-inspired bakes and craft projects.

Fiona teaches cake-decorating classes in south-west London, and has written and contributed to a number of baking and craft books and magazines. This is her second book.

Acknowledgements

Many thanks to everyone at Ivy Press, in particular to my editor Tom Kitch and to Wayne Blades and Simon Daley for the lovely design. A huge thank you to my project editor Jo Richardson, and to my wonderful photographer Sian Irvine and her assistant Joe Giacomet, who worked incredibly hard to capture the treats in their best light. Much love to all my wonderful friends and family for their support, and extra special thanks to my husband Dave for turning a blind eye to all the mess in the kitchen for months as I tested recipes, and for loving me through it all.

The publisher would like to thank:

Cheese Please
www.cheesepleaseonline.co.uk

Steamer Trading Cookshop
www.steamer.co.uk

Flint
www.flintcollection.com